JAMES MASON
ODD MAN OUT

SHERIDAN MORLEY

WEIDENFELD & NICOLSON
London

First published in 1989 by
George Weidenfeld and Nicolson Limited
91 Clapham High Street, London SW4 7TA

British Library Cataloguing in Publication Data
Morley, Sheridan, 1941–
Odd man out: the life of James Mason
1. Cinema films. Acting. Mason, James, 1909–
1984– Biographies
I. Title
791.43'028'0924
ISBN 0-297-79323-3

Printed in Great Britain by
Butler & Tanner Ltd, Frome and London

for Clarissa

Contents

Illustrations

ix

Acknowledgements

This biography was commissioned, like four others of mine, by John Curtis while he was at Weidenfeld & Nicolson, and equally patiently encouraged and supported by Larry Ashmead at Harper & Row in New York. I wrote and researched it over a three-year period from 1985 in England, Switzerland, the United States, Canada and Australia with unique and invaluable help from Mason's widow, Clarissa, and his elder brother, Rex. I would also like here to acknowledge the tremendous help of my wife Margaret, of Barbra Paskin who did many of the Los Angeles interviews, and of Sally Hibbin and her associates in London, as well as the eighty or so people listed in alphabetical order below, to all of whom goes my deepest gratitude for the time and trouble they took in answering my innumerable and sometimes impertinent questions, on tape or phone, or in letters or interviews, or with extracts from their own writing whether published or private:

Dennis Arundell; Frith Banbury; Janise Beaumont; Richard Benjamin; Joan Bennett; Ian Black; Amanda Blake; Pat Boone; Richard Brooks; Phyllis Calvert; Douglas Campbell; Dyan Cannon; D. F. Cheshire; George Christy; Robert Clark; Lee Van Cleef; James Coburn; Vivian Cox; Arlene Dahl; Ulf Dantanus; Diana de Rosso; Terence De Vere White; Edward Dryhurst; William Fairchild; Judith Fisher; Geraldine FitzGerald; Richard Fleischer; Robert Flemyng; Edward Fox; Ivan Foxwell; Sir John Gielgud; Milton Goldman; Morton Gottlieb; Ronald Gow; Stewart Granger; Donna Greenberg; Jane Greer; Dick Guttman; June Havoc; Patricia Hayes; David Hemmings; Buck Henry; Clive Hirschhorn; William Douglas Home; Hugh Hunt; William Hutt; Frances Hyland; Deborah Kerr; Perry King; Ted Kotcheff; Stanley Kubrick; Martin Landau; Janet

Leigh; Ruth Leon; Key Lenz; Sydney Lumet; Alex MacCormick; Roddy McDowall; Joe Mankiewicz; Roderick Mann; Sir John Mills; Helen Mirren; Robert Morley; Ronald Neame; Dan O'Herlihy; Graham Payn; George Peppard; Anthony Perkins; Christopher Plummer; Kay Pollock; Dilys Powell; Michael Powell; Lynn Redgrave; Madlyn Rhue; Stuart Rosenberg; Leonard Sachs; Jack Smight; Ray Stark; Rod Steiger; Andrew L. Stone; Beatrice Straight; Hunt Stromberg; Ann Todd; Bob and Catherine Victor; Alexander Walker; Eli Wallach; Kaye Webb; Stuart Whitman; Shelley Winters; Robert Wise; Michael York; Craig Zadan.

I am also deeply grateful to the librarians and staff of Marlborough College, the London Library, the British Broadcasting Corporation, the British Film Institute, the Academy of Motion Picture Arts and Sciences in Los Angeles, the Stratford Ontario Festival and the Performing Arts Research Library at Lincoln Center in New York, as well as to the editors and publishers of all magazines and newspapers and journals quoted in the text and to the authors and publishers of all duly acknowledged quotations.

Odd Man Out is dedicated to Clarissa Kaye Mason not because it is an 'authorized' biography, nor even solely because of her initial encouragement, enthusiasm and cooperation, but principally because it is what I believe James would have expected. But that does not mean any of the opinions in it are hers, except when expressed as such in direct quotation.

And lastly a word of great gratitude to my agent, Michael Shaw at Curtis Brown, without whom this book (like a dozen or so earlier ones of mine and countless hundreds of others) would never even have been started, and to Allegra Huston and David Roberts at Weidenfeld for seeing it safely through production and into the bookshops.

1

*'There have always been ups and down in my life, though
the downs do seem to have been more frequent than the ups.'*

WHEN, A YEAR or so after his death of a heart attack at the age of
seventy-five in the summer of 1984, I was starting to work on this
first biography of James Mason, I was in California and talking
about it over the phone (since she had declined a meeting) with his
first wife, Pamela. She viewed the book with severe misgiving, since
she felt it might conflict with a memoir of James that she and
her daughter, Portland Mason, were then planning. This was, I
gathered, to be a collection of his letters and drawings, together with
Portland's recollections of him in the early years of her childhood;
it would therefore have dealt with the postwar period before he left
his first family in Hollywood to return to Europe at the start of a
new life and then a new marriage in the 1960s. How, enquired
Pamela, would my book be any better than theirs?

I explained that my plan was to write a critical film biography,
covering the whole of James's life and career and not just the sometimes uneasy years he had spent as Pamela's husband and Portland's
father in a self-imposed but often unhappy Californian exile. I also
explained that I had been talking at some length to Mason's second
wife and widow, the Australian actress Clarissa Kaye, who had
shared the last fifteen years of his life and was kind enough to
encourage this book while commendably asking for no right of veto

1

or even consultation over the opinions expressed in it either by myself, or by others who had worked with James during his long career.

There was a long pause. Who else, enquired Pamela, apart from Clarissa, did I intend talking to about James? I said that these were still very early days, but that in writing several other stage and screen biographies over the last twenty years, from Noël Coward and Gertrude Lawrence through Sybil Thorndike and my grandmother Gladys Cooper to David Niven and Marlene Dietrich and Katharine Hepburn, I had usually found it necessary to talk to about a hundred friends, enemies and mere acquaintances of the subject in order to complete some sort of a jigsaw. There was another long pause, followed this time by a sudden burst of throaty laughter: 'A hundred?' echoed Pamela. 'You'll be lucky to find three.'

★   ★   ★

At first I thought she might have been right. Despite a considerable and often classic career of just over a hundred movies in fifty years, including such major works as *The Seventh Veil, Odd Man Out, Julius Caesar, A Star is Born, Lolita,* and the late glories of *The Verdict* and *The Shooting Party,* not to mention (as few ever did) some often equally intriguing stage work at the Old Vic and much later on Broadway, Mason seems to have created remarkably little impression on those around him on either side of the Atlantic, whether for good or for bad.

Interviewing him for magazines, newspapers, radio and television over the last decade of his life, I always thought he resembled some immensely courteous and urbane small-town doctor or solicitor: polite, considerate, charming, thoughtful, highly intelligent and reflective, but curiously remote about his career and his life, as though it had all been achieved at long distance by someone else, from some semi-detached transatlantic remove. He was like one of those characters in an early J. M. Barrie play who turns out to have wandered in from beyond the grave.

James seemed, even at the end of his life, not yet to have decided quite how he wanted to play himself. He was well into his seventies, and living through a time when most of his Hollywood-expatriate contemporaries, from Rex Harrison to David Niven, had long since given up playing anyone but themselves. In sharp contrast to them, he was always to remain the most intriguing and unpredictable of actors on screen.

What also separated Mason from most of the other British screen stars of his generation was that he always remained a craftsman actor rather than a gentleman player; one of the latter breed – my father Robert – remembers him through a couple of movies and ten years as an obsessive professional, inclined to be the only one on the set during lunch breaks, telephoning his agent to secure his next assignment with the minimum possible delay.

For all that, he hardly ever gave the impression that he had wanted or intended to be an actor in the first place. It merely became and remained his lifetime's work, one that he did to the very best of his abilities despite the fact that all his early ambitions had been for architecture.

There was a moment in his last starring movie, *The Shooting Party,* when he came up against Sir John Gielgud in a small role, and for a few brief screen minutes you could watch two great septuagenarian professionals, thirty years on from their *Julius Caesar,* but still at the very peak of their technical craft in front of the camera. The difference was that James never really understood quite how he'd got there, and was never entirely certain that it was his intended destination.

But before we go back to the very beginning, we had better perhaps recall something that his *Seventh Veil* discovery and co-star, the actress Ann Todd (whose long affair with Mason she only began to talk about for the first time when I interviewed her for this biography some months after his death), said to me:

'There was something electric and at the same time very dangerous about James, which had nothing at all to do with conventional screen stardom in postwar years. He was one of the few people who could really frighten me, and yet at the same time he was the most gentle and courteous of men. There was really no end to our love for each other, though I doubt we could ever have made a marriage work. In some ways we were far too alike, and I think he was always happiest alone, certainly until he found love and peace at last with Clarissa. What I always found so lovely and attractive about him was that sense of otherness, a sense that he'd really have been perfectly happy, as he once said to me, living as a guide in the Swiss mountains, or being an architect, or a painter, or even a gardener in Mexico.

'Acting was never the be-all and end-all of James's existence; indeed he often gave it hardly any thought at all unless a script happened to interest him intellectually. I don't really know what was the be-all or end-all of his existence, and maybe he didn't either, but I know what brought us together and held us together was an awareness of a life somewhere beyond the studios. We were both loners, and both of us often found that we weren't getting much love from anywhere else.

'James always found himself drawn in marriage to very strong and dominant women, but inside himself he was, I think, a little afraid of life, so he tended to float through it trying to avoid trouble wherever possible. In one sense, that could explain his pacifism during the war, though you might also argue that his was a brave stand to take when you consider how much harm it did his career and with his own family.'

The point about Mason is that whereas a contemporary like Niven couldn't live without people around him and something happening all the time, James had a zen quality of welcoming solitude and introversion. Contradictions and ambiguities were central to his nature: I believe he went to his grave still uncertain whether his conscientious objection to World War II had been an act of considerable isolationist courage or the appalling blunder of a coward. What is certain is that he was the finest actor of his generation on the British screen, and one of the very few who never allowed a sense of himself to get between him and his work.

Mason also brought a unique distinction to the postwar British cinema: coming immediately after a generation of officers and gentlemen and cads and bounders and silly asses on camera, he was perhaps the first truly adult actor, in a European sense, to make it to the top of his profession. For that reason, he was just about the only player in that league with whom French, German and Scandinavian actors wanted to work. Nobody, not even Jean Gabin or Max von Sydow, ever brooded on screen quite as well as Mason. Nobody before him had ever plausibly played a thinker in a British film except, possibly, Leslie Howard who always looked faintly embarrassed about his intellectualism. And nobody before Mason had ever so brilliantly conveyed, however innocently or unintentionally, a sense of such dark and almost mystic sexuality.

It was, therefore, with James Mason that the British cinema came of age: following the swashbucklers and the soldiers and the inane tennis-playing juveniles, James suggested something sinister, Continental and adult. His 'man you love to hate' roles all indicated, if not outright sexual or sensual perversion, then at least the possibility that sex and violence were intermingled with the strongest and most aristocratic love affairs.

Talking to him at the end of his life, when he was doing some of his finest work in films like *The Verdict* and *The Shooting Party*, James seemed to be looking back not in anything approaching anger but in courteous, mildly distanced regret. He had, in his own view and by his own admission, 'fucked up' his career by emigrating to America at the height of his British fame, and by continuing over there a futile battle against the big studios for control over his own movies and his own career, a control which he'd learned even in England could never be enjoyed by 'a mere actor'. The truth was that acting in other people's often undistinguished movies used to bore him rigid, but he lacked the financial or artistic energy to become the kind of autonomous director/producer/star that he most wanted to be, and occasionally attempted to be – with usually catastrophic results at the box office.

As a result, much of Mason's career was lived in a kind of academic sulk at the ways of a film world he neither fully understood nor ever much admired. He would, perhaps, have been at his happiest and most fulfilled had his own Cambridge University ever deigned to appoint a professor of film studies. As a man Mason was more academic, and as an actor more dangerous, than most studios could readily tolerate, and he therefore spent a lot of his time in a kind of internal exile.

If he had a major professional failing, it was perhaps only his absolute inability to hide from the camera the fact that he was usually more intelligent and intriguing than much of the scripted rubbish he was required to wade through while making a living. Thrice nominated for an Oscar (*A Star is Born*, *Georgy Girl* and *The Verdict*), he never actually won one. He remains, alongside Trevor Howard, one of the Academy's most shameful omissions, though it was not something that unduly concerned him. The reason for watching a James Mason film, as the film critic Pauline Kael once noted, was usually only James Mason himself.

5

For three consecutive years at the end of the war he headed all British box-office charts, and yet audiences at home took a long time to forgive what they saw as his desertion from the British film industry, coming so soon after what they saw as his desertion from the British Army in wartime. Those were the days when it seemed to Odeon audiences that a regular beating by Mason was a part of all desirable women's sex and social lives. His decision to abandon not only his home studios but also the semi-sadistic, intellectual roles that had made him so suddenly famous caused a kind of career confusion from which, professionally, he took several decades to recover.

In Montreal, during the 1967 World's Fair, they named him 'Cinema Actor of the Century'. The Canadians may well have got it right: certainly by the time of *The Verdict* fifteen years later, his corrupt, prince-of-darkness lawyer was giving even Paul Newman a lesson or two in the technique of screen survival. But there too Mason had been only second choice after Burt Lancaster, just as he had been second choice after Noël Coward for *Lolita* and after Cary Grant for *A Star is Born*. Yet time and time again, in such films and many more, he gave performances unequalled and unrivalled by those actors, or, for that matter, any other contemporary players. At this point, we had perhaps better go back to the very beginning.

2

'At Marlborough one was required to study and to play with virtue.'

JAMES NEVILLE MASON was born in Huddersfield in the West Riding of Yorkshire on 15 May 1909, the youngest of three sons of a reasonably affluent textile merchant. Almost eighty years later, talking to his eldest and by then only surviving brother Rex, I asked about the earliest memories of James and the family that he came from:

'We were really a very happy gathering of old Yorkshire stock, and our parents were first class; you simply couldn't fault them in any way. The family were cloth merchants, and father took the business over from his uncle, who was a bit of a fool, and turned it around into a considerable success mainly by going into the export trade, which meant he was always travelling around France and Belgium.

'So our mother was left to look after us three sons, but it was really a very happy and long marriage, right up to the diamond wedding when a local reporter in Huddersfield asked father if he'd ever thought about a divorce. "No," he said thoughtfully, "not a divorce exactly, but murder often." In fact they both lived to the age of ninety-two and got on quite remarkably well with each other: after mother died, father survived for a little while on gin and French cigarettes in the house they had shared for sixty-seven years.

'As boys we were all brought up by a wonderful governess called Miss Daft, who saw us all through to the same prep boarding school in Windermere; we were so close together in age, with only a year between each of us, that neighbours all thought of us as a sort of team though in fact we were very different. I was always set on the Navy, but by the time the First War had ended and I was thirteen there didn't seem to be much call for sailors. Colin, our middle brother, was talented but extremely lazy, always had to be beaten through his exams at school, and Jim was always the quiet one. He wasn't exactly a scholar at first, but he always did well enough at school and college, though as the years went by he seemed to grow increasingly distant and away from us, even before there was that terrible family split over his decision not to fight the war, after which none of us could really bring ourselves to speak to him for years.'

James joined his elder brothers, first at the Windermere prep school and then at Marlborough, where he seems to have worked his way adequately and diligently through the college, surviving within an alien community of hugely hearty sportsmen. In his own memoirs, published a few years before his death and charac-teristically remote even from himself, he writes with vague dis-affection of the school. He seems to have failed to notice that his time at the school in the mid-1920s coincided almost exactly with that of the poets John Betjeman and Louis MacNeice, not to mention the traitor Anthony Blunt and the actor James Robertson Justice, all of whom must have shared what Betjeman was later to encapsulate as his principal Marlburian memory: 'The dread of beatings, dread of being late, and greatest dread of all, the dread of games.'

According to Betjeman's biographer Bevis Hillier, the greatest possible sin at the school in that time was to be found guilty of 'coxiness' – or an undue desire to make some sort of impression on fellow-schoolboys. For this heinous crime Mason was once flung fully dressed into a swimming pool, so the self-effacement must have begun to vanish at some point in his Marlborough career.

His private energies at school seem to have been reserved for photography; he never acted in the occasional school plays, par-ticipation in which was usually limited to members of the upper-school French society, the Marlburian authorities presumably having decided that any kind of theatricality was essentially a foreign

8

affair. Instead James played, with increasing reluctance, the flute and rugby football.

Acting does not seem to have formed any part of Mason's school life, and there was certainly no early indication of any burning desire to take to the boards. He did, however, begin to develop a vague interest in the professional theatre of the London West End because his grandfather presciently formed the habit of sending him the *Play Pictorial* magazine every month. He did so not because of the theatre reviews, but because it published interesting photographs of actors and plays at a time when James was still taking some interest in the camera club at school, while also allowing a little light reading and suggesting that London might one day be worth a visit.

Those who were with Mason at Marlborough dimly recall an affable, rather unremarkable teenager with a faint inferiority complex from always being known as 'tertius' or 'minimus', this being the way that the third of three brothers at the same school was customarily addressed. But he worked reasonably hard, performed adequately in the classrooms and on the playing fields when required to do so (which was very often), and in fact was to do well enough in his final examinations to get a place at Peterhouse College Cambridge for the autumn of 1928, when he was nineteen years old.

Already, however, in his last years at school James was nurturing a faint sense of grievance about the way in which his life was shaping up. His father only agreed to pay for him through university on the strict understanding that he would afterwards choose a career with a guaranteed pension at the end of it. By 1926, his two elder brothers had left Marlborough and were being sent to language schools on the Continent, as their father wished them both to follow in his footsteps as distinguished travelling salesmen for the family textile business. But this was the time of the General Strike, and the very beginning of a worldwide depression that was to culminate three years later in the Wall Street crash. Inside the Mason family there was growing unease about the way their European export business was falling off and customers were suddenly failing to pay bills with their usual regularity. Against this climate, Mason's father began to face the prospect that there might be no room in the shrinking family empire for all three of his sons. As the youngest, James was the one selected not to be allowed to join.

At any rate, selected by his father: James's own views on the

9

subject seem hardly to have been canvassed at all, and it was perhaps not altogether surprising that relations between father and son should thereafter have begun to cool. The cataclysmic split came a decade or so later, with the war.

In the meantime, he continued in his last terms at Marlborough to keep a low profile, though as the present college librarian usefully notes, 'it would seem that the ethos of Marlborough in the Twenties tended to encourage anonymity'. It would be marvellous for a biographer to be able to note that such early proximity to Betjeman and Blunt had tended to encourage both the poetry and the secrecy that were to remain close to the heart and soul and character of James for the remaining years of his life, but alas there is no indication that their schoolboy meetings led to any such lasting influence.

An exhaustive trawl through school and house records of the period shows that Mason passed through the school almost without public trace, although he does make one archive appearance on the programme for a school concert of 30 June 1928, and a few months earlier he is mentioned in the *Marlburian* school magazine for taking part in a form debate on the motion 'That the present generation's taste in recreation typifies a general decadence'.

Proposing the motion, in what seems to have been his first and last major school speech, James asserted that 'the present age shows no sign of progress. The herd system of public schools is continued into other spheres, and checks the rise of great men. In pleasure alone are we not apathetic: recreation is the disposal of leisure, and leisure is the touchstone of character. Our leisure should be devoted to the perfection of our physical and mental powers, but the present generation seeks only for pleasure and finds that pleasure in sitting still, watching at theatres and cinemas and races and matches, instead of taking any active part. Professionalism has invaded our music, literature and sport, destroying all of their beauty.'

It is curiously typical of James's usually irritable personal philosophy that his first published and recorded words should form an attack on precisely those areas of professional entertainment where he was shortly to make his living. But at least his very first review was favourable: 'Mr Mason,' thought the notice for the debate in the *Marlburian,* 'contrived out of a mass of relevant and irrelevant facts and assertions to make a convincing speech.' And his closing address to the meeting was nothing if not boyishly theatrical: 'Mr

Mason rose to sum up: he acknowledged that we had made some progress since Elizabethan times, but considered that since the beginning of this century we had definitely degenerated. He concluded by dealing out abuse to his opponents all round. He then lost the motion by 102 votes to 2.'

So much for a career at Marlborough: Mason completed his final examinations, and left the school in the summer of 1928.

3

'The sense of freedom was exhilarating: Cambridge offered me, thank God, time and space in which to read and think about my circumstances and to figure out just who I was to be.'

IN CONSULTATION WITH his father and his Marlborough house-master, James had chosen to read Classics; not out of any abiding love for the subject but because, deprived of a place in the family business, it was generally agreed that the Indian Civil Service would be just the place for a chap like him. For that, a good Classics degree was still mandatory.

'Jim was still not really a scholar,' his brother Rex recalls, 'but he was the clever one of the family and Cambridge presented no real problems to him. In those days the Indian Civil Service was reckoned the thing to aim for if you were generally talented but without any very specific ambition, and Jim seemed reasonably happy to try for that at first, though I don't think his heart was ever really in it. At first, college life didn't seem to affect him very deeply, any more than Marlborough ever had; he just went along with it amiably enough, but he never really seemed to belong anywhere very much. Wherever you saw him, it was always as if he was just there on a sort of prolonged visit.'

In fact James took to the river, spending much of his time in the Peterhouse boats, and he made fleeting appearances at the Marlow and Henley regattas. Wondering, in later years, why he'd given up so much time to a fairly unintriguing and for him uninvolving sport, he concluded typically and philosophically that it must have been because he had read in some book that rowing had 'mystical and aesthetic appeal'.

At the beginning of his first summer term, everything changed more abruptly than his family might have wished. A rowing friend, Harry Gulland, introduced him into the world of college dramatics, and he made his first appearance in the chorus of a *Bacchae* directed by George Rylands, the legendary Cambridge don who had already tempted both the young Gielgud and the young Ashcroft from London into his Marlowe Society. This *Bacchae* was being performed under the auspices of the Cambridge University Football Club which was, curiously enough, expected to stage a Greek drama – preferably by Euripides – every third year.

Mason's arrival in the world of university theatre was not so much a matter of bursting onto the scene as of shuffling half-heartedly into the background of it. He felt that he had been sent to Cambridge to study rather than to act, and he was already deeply uncertain about what kind of future the stage could possibly offer him.

Nevertheless, an undergraduate start with Rylands was something an actor never forgot: 'Somehow,' wrote James years later, 'I got the impression that I was a success: whenever a gesture or a movement was assigned to a chorus individual rather than the group, then I seemed to be the one who got to do it. I was, you might say, the leader of the chorus.'

And the experience of a couple of choric nights in a Cambridge college garden seems to have been the most important of Mason's undergraduate career. He and Gulland had only applied for the roles 'for a bit of a lark', since they were both reading Greek and therefore knew the territory, but as a result of his success James began to think seriously about other college theatricals. 'It was partly this prominence, the fact of showing off on stage, that gratified my vanity. Somewhere in each unlikely chorus line there pants an ego equally confident of success.'

Mason's Cambridge acting career was, in fact, sparse to the point of minimalism: he did no theatricals at all in his second year and only two shows in his final one, although he had now made major decisions about his academic life and about his future. Somehow, the discovery of the theatre seems to have awoken in James, at last, a sense of his own independence and character. Witnessing not only that early Rylands production from backstage, but then, equally importantly, becoming a regular member of the audience for Terence Gray's professional theatre in the Newmarket Road, where some pioneering work was being done by a company rooted in German expressionism and heavily influenced by modern European drama in general, Mason had suddenly begun to realize that careers could be self-motivated.

Accordingly, towards the end of his first Cambridge year, he made two major if negative decisions: he no longer wished to read Classics, and he had no intention of making a life in the Indian Civil Service.

'Jim suddenly came home for that summer vacation,' recalls Rex, 'having decided that he would like to take up architecture. We never quite knew why, and I'm not entirely sure that he did, except that he'd heard very good things about the new Architecture School at Cambridge and was determined to give it a try. Father objected that he really couldn't keep chopping and changing his mind, but Jim was quietly determined to give up the Classics and so in the end that was that.'

In that first summer term at Cambridge, he had done all the work necessary to pass the first-year examinations in architecture, thereby ensuring himself two more years in the department of his choice. For a while he did not feel confident enough about his progress in the new discipline to allow himself any outside interests, not even rowing, and he still had to overcome a feeling, at least among his family in Yorkshire, that he was somehow rootless. 'Father always took the view', says Rex, 'that there was really no hope for him at all if he was just going to flit around from one possible career to another, which was probably why Jim eventually took so long telling him that he was giving up architecture too, in order to become an actor. As a young man, I suppose he did seem a bit rootless and uncertain of the kind of life he really wanted to lead.'

Nevertheless, in his third and last Cambridge year, which ended in summer 1931, James had the confidence to go back into student theatre, where, despite the presence of Michael Redgrave, the principal influence on him was now Dennis Arundell, the actor, director and teacher who was to achieve lasting fame as the original stage Lord Peter Wimsey in the Dorothy L. Sayers thrillers, a career he managed to combine with that of composer and Cambridge professor. In these undergraduate years that he shared with Mason, he had arranged the music for the Rylands *Bacchae,* and was now, in their third year, preparing to direct Purcell's *The Fairy Queen* for the Amateur Dramatic Society:

'I really can't remember the first time I met James at Cambridge, but suddenly he seemed to be hanging about backstage, and so I cast him as Oberon in the Purcell *Fairy Queen* which he also generously agreed to stage manage, admittedly rather chaotically as I don't think his talents lay in that direction at all. He was always a rather dreamy, likable chap, but with a terribly defensive barrier. There was no sign of much ambition, certainly not for acting, but I don't recall him ever talking about architecture very much either, though he did seem to be sketching quite a lot. The stage appeared to interest him up to a point, and he once asked me rather vaguely if I happened to think he could ever make it as a professional actor, and I remember trying to discourage him because he didn't seem to me to be all that good whereas there were at that time an awful lot of Cambridge graduates trying to make a go of it.'

Mason himself recalled *The Fairy Queen* experience as an expensive fiasco. Huge sets were miscued and crashed into each other, and he determined never again to be a stage manager. He was, however, still vaguely intrigued by the idea of acting, and went on from Oberon to a Marlowe Society *White Devil* in which he played Flamineo and drew a quite remarkable review from W. A. Darlington in the *Daily Telegraph.* This was not only Mason's first review, but also about the best he ever got as a stage actor in his entire career. Darlington did not much care for the production as a whole, but concluded his 1931 review: 'All but a few characters seemed to fade into the background, because the actors failed to define their outlines strongly enough. An honourable exception to this was the Flamineo: I cannot give the name of the actor playing this part, for the Marlowe Society preserve their anonymity, but I can say that I have not for some years seen at either of the great universities an actor with such a gift for sinister characterization. He spoke well, too.'

Spurred on by his first public acclaim, but unable to do anything theatrical about it, since his final architecture examinations were now looming, Mason returned to the drawing board and triumphed there too: only three first-class degrees in architecture were given by Cambridge in 1931, and James got one of them.

By now, however, Mason was only too aware of the gulf that lay between triumph in university life and employment in the real world. Just as he had begun to acquire confidence in himself as a photographer, he had joined the university's foreign film society and become aware through Eisenstein's *The Battleship Potemkin* and Carl Dreyer's *Jeanne D'Arc* of the greatness of visual composition beyond his reach. Just as he had begun to acquire confidence as a student actor, he had gone back to the professional Festival Theatre in Cambridge, now taken over by the young and brilliant Tyrone Guthrie, in time to see Robert Donat and Flora Robson demonstrating the gulf between college and real acting. And just as he acquired a first-class honours degree in the theory of architecture, he came down into real world gripped by a depression and disinclined to build anything at all.

James quite wanted to be an actor, and he quite wanted to be an architect: in the summer of 1931, he saw no realistic prospect of turning either of those still vague ambitions into a commercial career.

4

'The expensive meal of the day would be a meat pie from the coffee stall in Sloane Square.'

COMING DOWN FROM Cambridge, Mason reached a rapid decision: if he was to continue as an architect, he would have to go in for further studies. That would mean, unthinkably, asking his father to go on subsidizing him at the age of twenty-two, without any guarantee of employment even after the professional examinations which would take place in another two years' time. If, on the other hand, he became an actor, which he was beginning to think he might prefer anyway, there was a chance of immediate employment.

Accordingly, he took a shared room in Oakley Street, Chelsea, with a fellow Cambridge architecture First, Peter Megaw, and together they managed to pay the ten shillings a week rent out of money which they had been given by their families as twenty-first birthday presents.

Having virtually no other close friends in London, and nothing to do there except look for acting work, James spent the late summer and early autumn of 1931 trudging around stage doors and agents' offices, except on Thursdays when he would buy a copy of *The Stage* and religiously stay in Oakley Street writing off for any advertised jobs. Many prospective employers were impressed by Darlington's review in the *Telegraph,* and expressed the hope that Mason would indeed become a professional actor and return to them when he had

17

acquired some real experience. Quite how he was supposed to do that was never explained; but just as his birthday money was beginning to run out in the autumn, he finally got a reply to one of the hundreds of letters he had written to advertisers in *The Stage*.

A touring production was being sent out of *The Rascal,* and Mason was hired with almost suspicious speed on a first audition. He was to receive three pounds a week in return for playing the Russian prince who murdered Rasputin in a dramatization of the affair, which had to be loosely disguised as fiction in order to avoid legal wrangles with the prince's surviving family, who had already managed to extract several hundred thousand dollars from MGM for defamation. Mason's character was called Maritzi, Rasputin was called Karelin, and the play was enticingly billed as 'banned by the Lord Chamberlain' – which it once had been in London, on the tenuous grounds that it concerned distant relatives of the British royal family and was therefore unacceptable.

Nothing is certain in regional touring, however, and Mason soon discovered that not even his first-ever salary was guaranteed: the three pounds a week would be paid to him, but only if box-office takings could justify the expense. In towns where the take was not high, the cast's salaries would be correspondingly lowered – not that there were too many of these, since the producer doubled as author, the stage manager was a leading player, and the co-producer played Rasputin while his wife played the Czarina of all the Russias (except that she couldn't be called that for libel reasons, so she was called Czarina of all the Tintalians).

This somewhat hilarious venture, which Mason never read in its entirety since he was only given the pages of the script concerning his character, opened at the Theatre Royal in Aldershot, where he made his professional debut as an actor on 23 November 1931. It was also at that little-known theatre – this being a footnote for collectors of Hollywood trivia (or indeed my own biographies, where they are not one and the same) – that David Niven had made his first stage appearance while an army cadet at Sandhurst three years earlier. From Aldershot the tour proceeded to Tiverton in Devon, thence to Bath and north to Bilston, where the money ran out and the management disappeared by an early train one morning, leaving a somewhat rueful and still impoverished Mason to return home for a rather dour family Christmas in Yorkshire.

18

By now he did at least know that he was a professional actor, albeit a deeply unsuccessful one, and back in London early in the new year he managed to join a touring company run by Jevan Brandon Thomas, son of the author of *Charley's Aunt*. The company specialized in long summer seasons at seaside resorts. Among its other juveniles for 1932 were Patricia Hayes and Leonard Sachs, who recalls, 'a very nice, inexperienced, shy young man. I remember I had to put his make-up on for him because he had really no idea at all of how to do it. It was in some ways a rather gay company, but there was not a trace of that in James: indeed I remember him falling deeply in love in a rather hopeless and clueless way with Pat Hayes. He was like a young puppy, and a wonderful travelling companion as we toured around the country.

'The money was just terrible, three or four pounds a week, so for him and me the real treat was buying an expensive pack of cigarettes on a Friday night. He was always willing to learn about acting, but one never felt there was very much ambition there. He was a very accomplished artist, and drawing seemed to be his passion. Pat Hayes played all the young female roles from Peruvian vamps to the *Constant Nymph*, and James and I would alternate as her young men on stage and off; he was a sweet and gentle boy, somehow rather unworldly, and he certainly wasn't making any kind of a mark as an actor at that time. He would occasionally talk about Cambridge, or his desire to be an architect, with a sort of dry, self-deprecating humour, but I think he was already beginning to find in the theatre a kind of friendship and companionship that he'd never quite managed at school or college.'

For Pat Hayes, the most memorable thing about the Mason she knew in 1932, and was hardly ever to know again, was his utter indecisiveness.

'He'd ask you out for tea after the matinée, and when you agreed he'd look quite surprised and say, "Well then, where shall we go for it?" I discovered quite by chance, years later, that he'd once written to a friend saying that I was the first woman he ever thought about marrying, but it was typical of James that I never found that out from the man himself. I think he was rather unsure of his own sexuality at that time, or certainly of his own sexual power, and perhaps because I was very innocent too, I represented no kind of threat to him.'

19

Years later, Pat Hayes says, she used to gaze at Mason on the cinema screen and wonder why she had never fancied him at all as a young man: 'The camera did something marvellous for him, it seemed to light him up, whereas on stage he was really rather ordinary and desperately lacking in self-confidence. I was madly in love with Bernard Lee who at that time was very sparky, and compared to him James seemed oddly ill at ease both on stage and off. We used to do four or five different plays a week in each seaside town, so it was a marvellous training, but I can't remember that James really got very much better at it as the tour went on. I was very immature, too, but I was always rather forceful and I think James had rather a thing about very strong ladies, as his two marriages might suggest.

'Coming almost straight from university I was about the first working girl he'd ever met, and he seemed fascinated by that; he also once told my mother that I made him feel as if he could be a good actor on stage, but he was really only good in very stiff parts. He didn't seem to know how to loosen up, and offstage he was always terribly careful about money, counting the pennies for coffee out of his purse so slowly that you always felt obliged to offer to pay half.

'After the tour he used to drift into the Interval Club where we all tended to gather in London between jobs and he'd come over to my table and say rather self-consciously, "Would you like tea?" and if you agreed he'd say, "Well, where do you suggest we have it?" so you still had to make all the decisions yourself. He always waited for someone else to show him the way, as if he was a bit frightened of starting anything all by himself. He'd also been very sheltered by Cambridge and his Yorkshire background. I recall trying to introduce him to Louis Armstrong and jazz, which he absolutely hated. He was in some ways very conservative, and he said what he liked about me was that I was always so definite; he saw in acting some sort of escape from his upbringing, and although I think he knew at this time he really wasn't very good, he thought perhaps that he had a kind of personality which might be able to be developed in some way. He had a high level of social uneasiness which I think came from his own reticence. Once I remember some friend of his had asked him to look at her new baby, and James took me with him because he was terrified that he might say the wrong thing about it. There was something very endearing about his general hopelessness at that time, and I think looking back that he may have rather traded on that: women certainly always wanted to mother him.'

The Brandon Thomas season continued through the summer of 1932, moving along the south coast from Eastbourne through Brighton and Bournemouth to Torquay, with Mason cast as a series of minor juveniles and attracting an occasional local-paper reference to 'promising looks' or 'fine manliness and restraint'. But critics patently couldn't think of anything very much more definite to say about him as he turned up in *Old Heidelberg, The Torchbearers, John Ferguson, The Fanatics* and *At Mrs Beam's*, and all the other long-lost plays of English seaside repertory companies in those prewar years.

5

'No play in which I ever appeared in London or New York lasted more than three months, and most survived for a lot less time than that.'

SURROUNDED BY LEONARD SACHS and Pat Hayes and the other players of the Brandon Thomas company on tour, Mason found a kind of semi-student existence which his own shyness had prevented him from enjoying in his teenage years. He was now just twenty-three, still young for his age but so happy to have found some kind of regular, if only minimally profitable, occupation that even his disappointment at not having the money to continue his architectural studies began to fade into insignificance.

He was still sketching – actors' faces in rehearsal or landscapes discovered on long country walks – and for the rest of his life he was seldom to be at leisure without a sketchbook and a pencil. But even when, much to his regret, the Brandon Thomas tour came to an abrupt halt in the summer of 1932, there was no thought of going back to architecture. Instead he went straight to work for Billy Bell, Thomas's old stage manager, who was himself setting up a tour entirely devoted to the plays of Noël Coward. Mason later recalled, in a television documentary about the Master:

'Noël was then at the height of his fame, and he'd already, in his early thirties, written enough plays for an entire season to be made up of them. He appeared one morning at rehearsal in London, presumably to satisfy himself that the leading members of the touring

22

company were likely to perform adequately. The actors were in fact a spin-off from the Brandon Thomas company but for some reason Jevan wanted to lay off, and his stage manager decided to keep the company together only specializing in Coward plays ... I played all the rather dull young men, and the tour was an absolute disaster. At one point we decided it might help if we threw in two of the plays for the price of one in the same evening. The theatre was in a very bad way generally, with 'twofers' in London all the rage, whereby you got an extra ticket free, and we thought we were doing our bit on the road by offering a whole extra play for free, but that didn't work, either, and audiences stayed quite determinedly away from us in Exeter, Eastbourne, Brighton and Bournemouth. That poor stage manager was financially hit very badly, and Noël stayed well away from us too, though I think he once nodded politely to me in rehearsal. Certainly he wasn't heard to say anything witty on that occasion.'

After that uneasy start, relations between Coward and Mason were never to improve: a decade later Noël declined to cast James in his classic war film *In Which We Serve,* on account of Mason's avowed pacifism, and though both men were to spend their declining years within a few miles of each other above Lake Geneva, they resolutely remained on the most distant of terms.

Bell, the tour's manager, became a secondhand bookseller in the Charing Cross Road, and Mason returned to a London life that consisted largely of again tramping around agents' offices, while this time saving on the rent by staying with the mother of Dennis Arundell, his old Cambridge friend.

'We had an old house in Tottenham, and I remember mother sending James off to the Caledonian market with that very distinguished and unique speaking voice of his to purchase some oranges, so James would ask, "How much might these be?" in an impossibly elegant tones and then add "mate" in the hope of being taken for one of the locals. But he was never out of work for too long, and quite soon after that he got another job, up north.'

And this time not a tour, but a resident season with the repertory theatre at Hull, which was then being run by Michael MacOwan. James got off to a good start there, playing one of the leads in *The Prisoner of Zenda* (a script to which he was to return almost twenty years later in an appalling MGM remake of the original Ronald

Colman classic). After that the roles declined through the early months of 1933, until he found himself playing Second Warder in Galsworthy's *Escape* and reckoned the time had come to make his own escape back to London.

There he joined a rep in Croydon, hoping that at least he stood a better chance of being seen by London producers if he stayed vaguely within their geographic orbit. He got another crack at Coward (*Hay Fever,* again playing the rather unrewarding role of Sandy) before moving on to *Gallows Glorious,* a new play that Wendy Hiller's husband, Ronald Gow, had written about the American abolitionist John Brown and his raid on Harper's Ferry.

'I fear that wasn't a great success,' says Ronald Gow now, 'though we did transfer it to the West End and got some good reviews; it was the middle of a summer heatwave and no one came. Mason played one of the sons to Wilfrid Lawson as John Brown, and I seem to recall a rather likable young man, but with no trace of apparent future stardom. I do remember one terrible day in rehearsal when I thought the whole production would be coming to a grinding halt. Wilfrid Lawson was in the middle of a speech about where his march across America would take him and he was pointing at a map and Mason suddenly burst out into fits of giggles because Lawson was gesturing into the middle of Lake Erie. But we got over that one, Lawson was duly pacified, and the run staggered on. I always rather wished in later life that Mason had gone back to my play and taken the lead, as he really might have been very good by then. I fear most of us really didn't take quite enough notice of him in the theatre.'

That brief run of *Gallows Glorious* at the Shaftesbury in the summer of 1933 did, however, lead Mason on to the single most important engagement of his theatrical career: a knock on his dressing-room door in the last week announced the formidably tall presence of a director whose work Mason had last seen at the Festival Theatre in Cambridge. The director's name was Tyrone Guthrie, and he was about to start rehearsing a season at the Old Vic.

'Tyrone Guthrie carried around in his head an unusual casting directory, loaded with persons of unique personality and strange talent.'

GUTHRIE HAD HIMSELF only recently been summoned to the Old Vic by Charles Laughton. At the first great height of his screen fame as Henry VIII, he had agreed to return to the Baylis boards in the Waterloo Road, but only if Guthrie would take charge of the season. Now generally reckoned to have been the most inventive if unpredictable director of his generation (and one for whom Mason would return to work at Stratford, Ontario, twenty-one years later), Guthrie was assembling for the autumn of 1933 a quite remarkable company headed by Laughton and his wife Elsa Lanchester, and also featuring Flora Robson, Marius Goring, Athene Seyler, Leon Quartermaine, Ursula Jeans and Roger Livesey. The atmosphere backstage was, however, far from easy: Lilian Baylis – a legendary battle-axe whose most famous prayer was 'God send me good actors and send them cheap' and who, on being knocked down outside her stage door and hearing an ambulanceman say in awe 'It's Lilian Baylis of the Old Vic' arose to declaim '*and* Sadler's Wells' before relapsing into semi-consciousness – was less than happy at having her territory invaded not only by Guthrie but also by the despised 'West Enders', who would, she feared, fashionably follow a film star like Laughton to her Waterloo Road.

Mason presented no such stardom problems, and was offered a

rich and intriguing line of work to see him into his twenty-fifth year: at the Old Vic, James was to play Valentine in *Twelfth Night*, Yasha in *The Cherry Orchard*, Cromwell in *Henry VIII*, Claudio in *Measure for Measure*, Francisco (and understudy Laughton's Prospero) in *The Tempest*, Merriman the butler in *The Importance of Being Earnest*, Jeremy in *Love for Love* and Lennox in *Macbeth*, all between September 1933 and April 1934. This was in effect Mason's introduction to the classical theatre: although he had done a lot of Coward and some Galsworthy and Lonsdale on the road and in rep at Hull and Croydon, his post-Cambridge acting had otherwise been limited to one *Importance* (in which, at Hull, he played Algernon, a better role than Merriman) and one minor O'Neill. It was a gesture of considerable faith on Guthrie's part to invite him into so promising a season, even though he was relatively far down most of the cast lists.

James does not appear, however, to have lodged himself very deeply into Guthrie's consciousness: 'I engaged for small parts a young man called Mason' was all the director wrote in his memoirs of the Vic that season, though he did add later that James's Yasha, the valet in *The Cherry Orchard*, was 'a devastating sketch of Don Juan below stairs'. Mason himself seemed content to stand in the wings watching Laughton, the first great star he had seen at close range, and also a Yorkshireman, then fighting what the critic James Agate was to call 'a series of backdoor attacks on Shakespearean drama'. The productions met with mixed critical and public success, but they did serve to focus attention on the Vic again after a fallow period, and Mason came to the attention of Agate for 'leering his way successfully through Yasha'. Most of the other reviews went, naturally enough, to Laughton. Apart from the brief chance to take over as Prospero for a schools' matinée, Mason's chief benefit from the season was a sharp lesson from Charles ('a method actor without the bullshit', in his view) on keeping his make-up to a bare minimum.

This Old Vic winter also reunited James with Dennis Arundell, also making his debut there in small roles.

'That was perhaps when I got to know Mason best, because we were working together all the time for about nine months, and it was when I became aware for the first and only time that there might perhaps be a rather dark and moody side to James's otherwise tranquil nature. One evening we were back at my flat after the show, and James sat rather aloof because he really wasn't a very good mixer. But that night Ursula Jeans went on and on at him about being so stand-offish, and suddenly James got up and disappeared from the room. We went out to look for him in Leicester Square thinking he'd probably gone out to pick up a tart or something like that. But we couldn't find him, so we went back to the flat only to discover that James had got there before us and again Ursula started at him about being so distant. Suddenly James leaped up and seized her by the throat and really began to shake her; but Ursula was very tough and saw him off, and after that we all made it up and went to Lyons Corner House for eggs and bacon at about three in the morning. But in that one moment I suddenly saw there could be something rather violent and unpredictable about James when he really got angry or challenged.'

The Old Vic season continued quietly enough, with the added bonus that because of Laughton the film producer Alexander Korda would come to all the first nights, scouting out other talent for his Denham Studios. In that way Roger Livesey landed a major role in Laughton's next film, *Rembrandt*, and James was given a week's work in *The Return of Don Juan*, which was to star Douglas Fairbanks, Sr, in a latter-day return to one of his most famous swashbucklers.

Before that could get under way, however, Mason had to consider his theatrical future. The Laughtons were quitting the Old Vic at the end of the season and, although James had graduated to one or two good supporting roles, there was no doubt that among the juveniles it was Roger Livesey who had attracted most of the attention, leaving Lilian Baylis with no particular desire to re-engage Mason for another year. But now he had come to the attention of John Gielgud, who was about to direct a play in the West End about Mary Queen of Scots, written by the 'Gordon Daviot' who had recently given him a huge and career-shaping success as *Richard of Bordeaux*.

In the title role of the doomed Queen, Gielgud had cast Gwen Ffrangcon-Davies, his co-star from *Bordeaux*, and the young Laurence Olivier was to play Lord Bothwell. Mason was given two relatively minor roles: a French valet and one of Mary's Scots suitors. Felix Aylmer and Margaret Webster were also in a strong cast, but as Gielgud later noted 'the play was very uneven, and so was my production'. Olivier was accused by at least one critic of playing

27

Bothwell 'with all the mannerisms of Clark Gable', and although two great directors, George Devine and Glen Byam Shaw, also turned up with Mason in minor roles, the production is mainly remembered by its survivors for the vast amount of food and drink that was consumed backstage during some of its longer duologues.

After another very short summer in the West End (*Queen of Scots* ran little longer than *Gallows Glorious* had the previous year), Mason was now understandably eager to embark on a whole new career as a film actor. There was Korda's promise of a debut in the Fairbanks *Don Juan*, though this too proved to be something of a disaster. Mason had been contracted for seven days' work as a young stud who gets killed by mistake early in the proceedings. He took an instant dislike to the elder Fairbanks, still laboriously re-enacting the stunts that had made him famous twenty years earlier, and the dislike seems to have been mutual. Korda himself was directing the early sequences from behind a much-perused copy of *The Times,* and after about three days' work it was gently indicated to Mason that perhaps a mistake had been made about his casting. The seven days shrank to three, the part was recast, and Mason left the picture in a haze of gentlemanly regret. *The Return of Don Juan* was not an auspicious opening to one of the most distinguished acting careers in the history of the cinema, and James rapidly returned to the theatre whence he had so recently come.

7

*'Al Parker always said I first looked at him as though he
had just pissed down my leg.'*

IN THE AUTUMN of 1934, John Gielgud, who had so recently
directed Mason in *Queen of Scots*, was planning to return to the Old
Vic as Hamlet with Jessica Tandy as Ophelia, her future husband
Jack Hawkins as Horatio, and Alec Guinness as Osric. It was to be
a starry revival, the key Shakespearean production of its period
according to some critics, though one or two others still thought
it 'Everest half-scaled'. James was offered either Rosencrantz or
Guildenstern, whichever might take his fancy.

It was a tempting offer, and Mason was tempted: but he had
already done a season of small Shakespearean roles at the Vic, and
didn't altogether fancy another. Moreover his abrupt dismissal from
the Korda picture, and his appalling luck in West End runs, was
beginning to suggest that perhaps his actor's training was still in
some way deficient, and that he had better find himself some further
experience in one of the more distinguished regional repertories
rather than content himself with another winter of glorified spear-
carrying over Waterloo Bridge.

Accordingly he auditioned for the Gate Theatre in Dublin, then
being run (in flamboyant opposition to the Abbey) by Micheal
MacLiammoir, a child-actor contemporary of Noël Coward in
London who had recently set up in an Irish management with his

lover Hilton Edwards. The two men were now in urgent need of a leading actor for the autumn season at the Gate, having just lost the young Orson Welles to New York. They were keen to cast a Brutus as soon as possible.

MacLiammoir, who with Edwards ran one of the gayest theatre companies that even Dublin in its sexual and social tolerance had ever known, unsurprisingly fell immediately under the spell of James's saturnine good looks and dark-treacle voice. 'In London,' as he later wrote, 'we engaged a young actor called James Mason whose icy English smile froze my heart, but whose Brutus I admired immensely.'

In addition to starring in *Julius Caesar* that autumn at the Gate, almost twenty years before he was to play the same role on screen opposite Gielgud and Brando, Mason also took on leading roles for MacLiammoir in the *The Provok'd Wife*, *The Drunkard*, *Othello* and Chesterton's *Magic*, beginning for the first time to find his feet as an actor and to lose some of the coltishness that had proved so limiting until now. When I spoke to MacLiammoir years later about his memories of the Gate, he said that James's greatest asset was his voice, which James himself always thought too flat and soft, and his greatest drawback was a habit of coming on stage looking as though he might be found out and sent back to some completely different career.

Mason found Dublin 'a city that encourages bitchiness', but all remained relatively harmonious at the Gate, despite Micheal MacLiammoir's insistence on playing Mark Antony dressed from head to toe in leopardskin, and despite the fact that the local critics, ever eager to mock Micheal's turbulent theatricality, began lavishing praise on the visiting Mason rather than on the captain of the home team.

While in Ireland James went to live in the family home of the author and literary editor Terence de Vere White:

'I was then a Dublin solicitor, and having met James at a party I told him there was a spare bed in my mother's house: he was a tall, dark and slim man, desperately worried about whether he had enough talent for the theatre. To cheer him up I told him that if all else failed he could always turn to films and become the English Clark Gable, but he said there was nothing he would want to do less than that. He was very taken at the time with a Gate actress called

Ria Mooney, but I doubt anything very much ever came of it as she was highly religious.

'I can't think of an actor who changed less in the course of a whole career. The Brutus he played on film in Hollywood was exactly like the one he played at the Gate all those years earlier: a quiet, thoughtful, meditative performance. I think Micheal and Hilton were quite fond of him, but the year before they'd had Orson Welles and he was the one they really loved, especially in later life when Welles became rather useful in finding them film work. James never quite managed that, and he remained very separate, very much his own man. Micheal was of course desperately jealous of his looks, but not I think of his acting: after Welles, he seemed somehow a little tame.'

Early in the new year of 1935, Mason played Heathcliff in *Wuthering Heights* at the Gate (one of the many good roles he was to lose on screen because of Olivier's more rapidly established Hollywood stardom) and then the male lead in *Lady Precious Stream*, before deciding that he had been the big fish in a small pond long enough, and it was time to have another crack at London. James's decision to return to the West End was also encouraged by the vague promise of a job as Prince Albert in a new play about Queen Victoria, which would have to be performed in a club theatre because of the scandal attached to putting recent royalty on stage. But in the time it took him to get back from Dublin, the management had come across Vincent Price, a young actor who had been studying art in Germany and therefore arrived complete with the correct accent for Albert. Mason was once again out of a job. Unemployment this time lasted right through the summer of 1935, and James spent some of this period re-establishing contact with his brother Rex:

'I used to pass through London occasionally, travelling for the family firm, and when James was unemployed I would take him out and make sure that he got at least one decent meal a week. He and I would spent the evening together and I remember being quite shocked sometimes by the state of his digs and the rooms he was having to live in. I hardly ever saw him act, though after *Queen of Scots* I remember him taking me to meet the star, Gwen Ffrangcon-Davies, and my telling her that it was a thoroughly decent show, which he said later wasn't quite the level of praise she was accustomed to. Another time he took me to lunch with the Laughtons, and there was an admiral's daughter James was for a while quite

31

keen to marry, but I don't think her family really approved of unsuccessful actors.'

All that was, however, just about to change. Towards the end of the summer of 1935, with still nothing on the horizon, Mason went to a cast party on the stage of the Lyric Theatre. Another of the guests was the American agent and director Al Parker. Al had started out in America as an actor, and then he directed Fairbanks in *The Black Pirate*. When the Crash came he took a job with Twentieth Century Fox directing studio tests, and they sent him to London to work on the casting of *Cavalcade*. Once there he set up a studio for Fox, fell in love with the country and never went back. But the most remarkable thing about him was that he had an immediate eye for talent, and on stage at this party he suddenly saw James across a crowded set and wouldn't give anyone any peace until they introduced him. James's usual reticence made him seem to Al terribly rude, but eventually Al broke down all the barriers and asked Mason to audition for him. At that time Al was directing a series of what they called 'quota quickies', low-budget pictures made very rapidly to satisfy a government ruling that a certain number of the films shown in British cinemas every week had to have been made inside the country rather than shipped over in cans from Hollywood.

Mason was at this time uncertain that he ever wanted to see the inside of a film studio again, recalling only too vividly his ignominious sacking by Korda, an episode he had thought it wisest not to mention to Al Parker. His future agent, manager, friend and director found out about it soon enough, but remained confident that he had also found a film star just waiting for the right film. Or, in the absence of the right film, any film that happened to be available at the time. Within a matter of days Parker had given Mason a screen test, extracted him from a loose agreement with the agent who had organized his *Don Juan* contract, signed him with Fox, and given him the role of a cub reporter in the picture he was currently shooting for Fox's English division at Wembley. Thus it was that, in the autumn of 1935, James Mason made his screen debut in a film called *Late Extra*.

*'I began to fear that the movie world had no more to offer
me than endless travel between Wembley and Walton-on-
Thames.'*

'HIS ACTING IS adequate, though far from outstandingly good,'
wrote a trade paper critic of James's debut performance as the cub
reporter in *Late Extra*, thereby giving him his first-ever review as a
movie actor and, incidentally, setting the tone for a great many more
to follow. Mason was still very dubious about his prospects in films,
and with some reason: though he had begun to develop that deep
velvet voice and gentle delivery which would successfully cover his
Yorkshire vowels, his manner on screen was uneasy. But as the
actress Joan Gardner had said to him after his Korda sacking: 'Never
mind and don't take it too hard, I was terrible in my first films too.'

Now, however, he had at least managed to complete one, although
to suggest that *Late Extra* failed to take the British moviegoing
public by storm would be like suggesting that the Sahara can get a
little dry. The film hardly seems to have taken its public by anything
at all: its plot lasted a mere sixty-five minutes, which was the time
it took Mason to locate a murderer while also getting himself roman-
tically involved with another reporter on the paper. Virginia Cherrill,
the first Mrs Cary Grant and remembered as the blind girl in
Chaplin's *City Lights* but now slithering down through British B
movies on her way to becoming (albeit briefly) the Viscountess
Jersey, played the other reporter. The film crept into the lower half

of double features at a few cinemas, though not many of its supporting cast (a distinguished line-up of Alastair Sim, Cyril Cusack, Michael Wilding and Donald Wolfit) could later recall having made it at all.

But what Al Parker was now offering Mason, at a time when precious few offers were coming from elsewhere and none at all from the West End, was roughly the equivalent of another season in rep, though playing to cameras instead of regional audiences and for vastly better money: sixty or seventy pounds a week instead of the twenty or thirty he had been getting at the Old Vic. These quota quickies had by their very nature to be made at the rate of at least two a month, and Parker was in the habit of shooting them back-to-back, cutting his schedules and therefore his overhead costs so fine that if a film overran by even a day or two he would simply shoot all through the night in order to make up time before the sets were struck to make way for the next picture.

Moreover, the contract he had made between Mason and Fox was such that, if they had nothing suitable for Mason at Wembley, he could be loaned out to Walton-on-Thames where other quota quickies were being made by George Smith, including one called *Twice Branded* in which James made his second screen appearance, this time playing the snobbish and unforgiving son of an ex-convict (Robert Rendel) who returns from jail to try and rebuild a family life. The only critic to review James in this one, again for a trade paper, found him 'rather too stagey'.

Then it was back to Wembley for his third picture, his second with Al Parker and one that was to change his private as well as his public life forever. Prophetically entitled *Troubled Waters*, this was another hour-long quickie in which James was to play a government agent on the track of some explosives smugglers. Mason was reunited with Alistair Sim and Virginia Cherrill from *Late Extra*, only this time the cameraman was to be Roy Kellino, a talented young cinematographer who was married to the former Pamela Ostrer, daughter of a wealthy executive at the Gaumont-British film company, and, like James, the descendant of a north-country textile family.

Pamela was a formidable and intelligent beauty who had been one of the child discoveries at Gaumont-British and played the daughter in *Jew Suss*. Now that she was married to Kellino, her main concern was getting him home at night and away from the round-the-clock shooting schedules imposed by Al Parker in his increasingly desperate attempts to get the quota quickies to live up to their name. One night, when shooting was threatening to go way past midnight on the *Troubled Waters* set, Pamela appeared to collect her husband.

Quite what happened then is uncertain. James, in his characteristically clenched and embarrassed way, even at the very end of his life, some fifty years later, wrote only that 'I was very attracted to Pamela, and went to live with her and her husband for several years before we were married'.

By now an established bachelor in his middle twenties, and characterized by a lifelong Yorkshire caution about spending money even when he had any, Mason had long since taken the view that borrowing or renting rooms in the flats and houses of his married friends and acquaintances was a great deal less trouble and less costly than setting up an apartment of his own. He was staying with friends when he first met Pamela on the *Troubled Waters* set, and he encouraged them almost at once to ask her round for a party, so keen was he to renew her acquaintance. Soon after that, Mason began lodging with the Kellinos, an arrangement that was to last through the late 1930s. As the director, Ronald Neame, recalls:

'When eventually, at the beginning of the war, Kellino announced that he was moving out of the marital home and getting a divorce citing James, it didn't cause too much surprise, although their life as a trio did seem to have been going on for such a long time by then. You'd see them together at parties, and for a while they even formed their own kind of private family film unit, with Pamela (who was a talented novelist) doing the writing and James acting and Roy directing.'

It was all amicable enough, at least in the early days, as James went on in rapid succession to two more undistinguished quickies, *Prison Breaker* for Adrian Brunel and *Blind Man's Buff* again for Al Parker. Parker by now was billing him in some desperation as 'Britain's Biggest Box-Office Bet', even though it was one that few appeared to be taking. One critic did get as far as calling him 'daredevil and amusing' on screen, but Mason realized after starring in four or five of these undistinguished little thrillers that he was in severe danger of losing whatever credibility he had gained from the seasons at the Old Vic and the Gate. He therefore faced a career choice: either to get back into the theatre, where he always secretly thought he belonged, or to get into a better class of film than those being shot by Al Parker at the rate of two per month.

First he tried the theatre again. He had made one brief return to the Croydon Rep in 1935 for *The Abbé Prévost* but now, encouraged by his old friend Leonard Sachs, who had begun putting on plays at the Arts Theatre Club, he and Pamela went briefly into a curious little Hungarian musical called *Luck of the Devil* which Pamela part-financed and which was designed to prove that, despite Kellino's considerable doubts, she could make it as an actress.

With that theory still unproved, Mason went for a week or two back to MacLiammoir at the Gate in Dublin to play in *Parnell*, but there still seemed no real interest or focus in his theatrical career. And the money was in movies, if only he could find something a bit classier than the Wembley quickies.

After one more of those (*The Secret of Stamboul*, in which he played a Guards officer quelling a little local uprising, and was hailed by *Kine Weekly* at least as 'a young hero of promise'), Mason found the courage and the opportunity for a break with Parker and the low-budget Wembley life. It appeared that National Provincial, not the bank but a slightly richer film-making outfit than Parker's, was about to shoot *The Mill on the Floss*, John Drinkwater's screenplay of the classic George Eliot novel with a starry cast headed by Fay Compton and Griffith Jones. Mason was offered the role of Tom Tulliver, and saw at once that he had to do it if he was ever to gain any kind of screen respectability.

Accordingly he begged his studio masters at English Fox to give him the kind of loan-out they had allowed to the studios at Walton. Fox agreed to it, much to the rage of Al Parker, who not only wanted Mason for another quickie but saw this as a betrayal by the actor he had discovered and nurtured for the last eighteen months. For the next two years the two men did not speak, and as it turned out *The Mill on the Floss* was not such a good idea after all. Despite its distinguished literary pedigree the picture kept running out of money, with the result that its director, Tim Whelan, returned to America halfway through the shooting, leaving a certain amount of chaos behind him.

The actress Geraldine Fitzgerald, who played Mason's sister in *Mill on the Floss*, remembers now 'a desperately attractive young man. I recall telling him that one day the camera was going to love him and make him a very great star, and James just continued to look at me in disbelief. He was incredibly good-looking, in a dark sort of way. I remember in Dublin when he was at the Gate there were great rumours of a romance with Iris O'Callaghan, but I think at this time he was already getting very fond of Pamela. He had that curious quality of a man with an eternal secret; like Charles Laughton on screen, he could seem to be thinking about two quite different things at once; he was always on a double track, and that was what was so arresting and incredible about him. That and I guess the voice. We sort of limped through the picture together, with the money falling apart all round us, but I don't think James had any real notion of what he was going to be on screen, or how successful. He was just there doing the job.'

9

'The ease that I instinctively knew was essential to good film acting was initially quite beyond my reach.'

BY THE END of 1936, Mason's career was still in bad shape. He had been a professional actor for five years, had achieved promising work in two resident seasons at the Vic and the Gate, but otherwise done little of note in the theatre; on screen he had made seven movies, all but one a quota quickie and that one nearly destroyed by the financial chaos surrounding its shooting. Screen acting appeared to be a matter of hitting marks and collecting paycheques whenever possible. It had none of the intellectual excitement of the theatre, or even the more immediate rewards of the architectural drawing board, which he still yearned back to (as he would for the rest of his life) in moments of professional despair about the curiously shaky profession he appeared to have chosen for himself.

Predictably, he now began to spend more and more of his spare time with Pamela: not only was she precisely the kind of strong, intellectual, self-willed woman he had always found most attractive, she was also a writer and a thinker who shared his general distaste for the banalities of film-studio chatter. She seemed to be taking an almost proprietorial interest in the direction of his career – or, rather, the current lack of it. In November 1936 they made their second stage appearance together in a script they had jointly written, entitled *Flying Blind*. For those already intrigued by their relationship, the

play's short life at the Arts Theatre gave further cause for speculation: directed by Pamela's husband, it told the story of a married
women falling in love with an airline pilot, and was immediately
denied a West End licence by the Lord Chamberlain because the
woman's young sister was reckoned to be a 'voyeur' of their relationship.

Around this time Mason also made his first appearance in a film
of any distinction, and in a significant part, though all too typically,
given his current screen luck, he went unbilled and uncredited for
the work. At the very beginning of Korda's *Fire Over England*, the
film in which Laurence Olivier plays a dashing Englishman who
helps Flora Robson's Queen Elizabeth to forecast and crush the
Armada, there is an English spy in the employ of Raymond Massey's
Spanish King, a spy who gets killed early in reel one thereby allowing
Olivier to take his place. It is Mason who plays the spy, in an
elegantly pointed beard but with total anonymity on the cast list,
presumably because he had only a couple of days' work and nobody
bothered to keep an accurate record of the bit-players.

For the other films he was making, as 1936 turned into 1937,
Mason was given rather more credit, but might from the reviews
have wished for anonymity there too: critics who had found *The
Secret of Stamboul* 'foully acted and cinematically still in the egg-
laying stage' thought not a lot better of *The High Command*, a
Thorold Dickinson drama in which he again wore a Ronald Colman
moustache that had a habit of appearing at totally different lengths
in succeeding scenes. As the film was largely shot in close-ups of
Lionel Atwill playing a military man, Mason and his co-stars took
irreverently to calling it *The General Has No Legs*. Studio publicists,
desperate to arouse local distribution interest in yet another Mason
turkey, sent it out with a series of suggested captions, ranging from
'a gripping story of love and hate in an outpost of Empire' through
'the shadow of a man's past threatens to ruin those he loves' to
the epic 'love, murder, hate, jealous passions all unleashed on the
mysterious coast of West Africa', and throughout England audiences
once again stayed away in their thousands.

Back in the theatre, James and Pamela travelled to Ireland early in
1937 to appear at the Gate, James's old home ground, in a dramatization of *Pride and Prejudice*. In London, however, there was

still no real demand for him as a stage actor. Indeed, the impresario Henry Sherek remembered trying to find a leading man for Luise Rainer, then at the height of her movie fame and eager to do a new play in the West End. He hit upon the idea of Mason and sent him to see Miss Rainer. But she rejected him for the part and it was to be another eight years before movie audiences around the world began to think she might have missed something.

But it started to dawn now, on both James and Pamela, that something drastic had sooner or later to be organized: not only were they not getting much work as a stage team, but James's movies were going from bad to worse at a time when the entire British film industry was doing much the same. Mason, who unlike many of his generation spent large amounts of time thinking about the nature, perils and possibilities of the British cinema, and usually got himself into trouble for voicing such thoughts when actors were meant to shut up and take the money, decided in March 1937 to write to a movie magazine advocating a major shift in British film policy.

'If we are ever to compete seriously with Hollywood,' he wrote, 'we shall only do so by improving the standards of our cheap and unpretentious films [precisely those he had been making for the last two years] and forgetting our extravagant endeavours to capture the world market with super productions [in only one of which Korda had ever asked him to participate]. The cheap film should then have as much chance of world release as any colossal masterpiece, provided that sufficient attention is paid to the story and the writing of the dialogue, and to the casting of small supporting parts.'

As a masterplan for a better film future it could have been worse, except that by 1937 the British film industry was in such artistic and economic disarray that it scarcely had the time to listen to one small-time actor bitching from the sidelines, however accurately. James's fate was always to be a prophet without much honour around the studios, and a large part of his career frustration then and later stemmed from a desire, only semi-articulated, to have more control over his own artistic destiny than he would ever manage to organize.

Even within his own small world at the Fox British studios in Wembley, he was already unpopular. The more he complained about conditions there the less anyone else, with the possible exceptions of Pamela and Roy Kellino, valued his contributions to movies that were still signally failing to make a mark. It was for Kellino as director that James made the last of his Fox quickies (*Catch as Catch Can*, an American jewel-robbing caper in which Mason and Vicki Dobson could not hope to acquire the Hollywood high-society charm of William Powell and Myrna Loy, although the film did at least give Margaret Rutherford a start). He then went straight back to Korda for *The Return of the Scarlet Pimpernel*.

This was an attempt to cash in on the success of the Leslie Howard/Merle Oberon/Raymond Massey classic of two years earlier with a very much cheaper cast (Barry K. Barnes/Sophie Stewart/Henry Oscar), and the result was predictably derided by many critics: 'Same old Guillotine Square' thought the *New York Times*; 'same old aristocrats dying with incredible grace, same old extra-women knitting and cackling obscenely as heads fall, same old British melodrama laid on with fine old British unrestraint. Credit is due to both director and cast for betraying so few signs of ennui.'

James despaired of getting anything better, and by now the Fox studio at Wembley had failed to offer him another contract even in London, even while moving such fellow contract-artists as George Sanders and Patrick Kowles to the home base of California. Mason therefore decided to have one more major attack on the London theatre. Between March and September 1937 he appeared in four productions, each of which proved true to his conviction that he would never see a long run on any West End stage.

First came *The Road to Rome*, Robert Sherwood's Hannibal play which at least got his name up in lights outside the Savoy Theatre, though not for long; then came *Miserable Sinners* at the Ambassadors, a play written especially for Pamela and James by his fellow-Cambridge undergraduate of a decade ago, the thriller writer Nigel Balchin. After that there was a curious little play at Kew about a lunatic, the title of which even Mason managed to get wrong in his memoirs (it was called *A Man Who Was Nothing*), but then came, at last, one that really did look like a winner: Dodie Smith's *Bonnet Over The Windmill*. Miss Smith had lately enjoyed West End successes with *Autumn Crocus* and *Call It A Day* and there was nothing, apart from James's usual theatrical ill-fortune, to suggest that her new backstage romantic comedy would not complete the hat trick.

In the event, it did nothing of the kind: the H. M. Tennent management assembled an intriguing cast (Cecil Parker, William

41

Douglas Home and Ivy St Helier) but Miss Smith took an early dislike to James.

'I was extremely worried about him at the play's first reading. It wasn't merely that he read badly: it almost seemed as if he couldn't read at all, although after a few rehearsals he began to give indications of being excellent.'

That was more than critics thought of the play, however. David Fairweather, the *Theatre World* reviewer, having predicted 'a brilliant future' for Mason after his appearance as Hannibal a few months earlier, was now complaining about 'very curious intonations that sometimes mar his diction'. Only the actor William Douglas Home, soon to become a playwright himself, seemed to notice that there might be more to James than immediately met the eye.

'I found watching him at rehearsals a fascinating experience ... I was able to detect a variety of tone, and a kind of withdrawn sincerity and sensibility, which as I listened to him day by day enthralled me ... When we came to perform the play, I fear that Mason's quiet, naturalistic style was not appreciated by the audiences, still less by the critics. Indeed I recall one critic saying Mr Mason was positively rude to his audience. For my own part I suspected that he was not being deliberately rude, but merely acting on the stage in the convention to which he was best suited, and in which he was so soon to make his name.'

Bonnet Over The Windmill just made it from September through to Christmas 1937, whereupon James and Pamela decided that if no one was going to offer him another film, they had better create one of their own.

10

'The writing that Pamela and I did together was almost invariably based on an idea which made a vertical take-off from the top of her head.'

'ONE OF THE things you have to understand about James in these late 1930s,' says the actor Robert Flemyng, who was to remain a lifelong friend and whose wife Carmen was a witness at the eventual wedding of James and Pamela in February 1941, 'is that there were only two people alive who thought he had the faintest chance of becoming a world star, and neither of them was James himself.'

One of those people was Al Parker, with whom James had not spoken since the row about his departure from Wembley for *Mill on the Floss*; the other of course was Pamela. 'Coming as she did from a family of studio executives,' says Flemyng, 'she had a strong sense of film which James lacked. He was always very dismissive, and usually rightly, of the B pictures he was still making, the ones that were shown just to fill up the home-made quota at Odeons. Audiences were so used to them being terrible that as soon as the opening credits came up they used to sit there chanting, "Take it off, it's British", and James would quite often join in, even when it was one of his own films.

'He was always cynical and aloof about his work whereas Pamela was much more openly ambitious, which is perhaps why she went on acting even after the war though she was really pretty bad at it.'

She did, however, have other talents, and began around this time

43

to make a certain name as a novelist. As far as James was concerned – currently without an agent or manager and drifting around in a haze of minor movies and shortlived plays – Pamela decided that matters would have to be taken into her own hands.

What she now had was the idea for a film, one which would in many intriguing ways foreshadow by eight years the *Odd Man Out* with which Mason did finally achieve screen greatness. Hers, too, was the story of a fugitive on the run from justice: in this case the runner was a young farmer who kills his nagging and ill-tempered wife and then falls in love with a young novelist, only to discover that she is writing about his true identity; fleeing again, he is chased into the sea and drowns in a conclusion only faintly less melodramatic than that of *A Star is Born* fifteen years later.

Given that no studio was showing much interest in James at the time, let alone a project as apparently downbeat as this (the first title, only changed close to distribution, was *Deadwater*), Pamela decided that the only sensible way to make it was as a virtual home movie: she and James would co-script and star as the murderer and the novelist, her husband would produce and direct, and the cast would be made up of theatrical friends offered a few weeks at their country cottage in return for some acting. To save further costs, most of the picture would be shot silent, on film stock that they managed to buy up cheaply as 'leftovers' on the end of used reels, and then post-synchronized later.

Soon after Christmas 1937, just after the closing of *Bonnet Over The Windmill*, James and Pamela retired to Wengen in Switzerland to write what would become the screenplay for *I Met A Murderer*, the film that was to occupy them and Kellino for almost the whole of 1938. Roy was also principal cameraman, since every possible cost was being saved, though he did have a promising young assistant called Oswald Morris. The total budget was just under five thousand pounds, skeletal even for the late Thirties, and the only actors to get any kind of money were William Devlin who played the suspicious farmhand, and Sylvia Coleridge (who had been with James in the Hull Rep) as the nagging wife, though Peter Coke and one or two others from *Bonnet Over The Windmill* joined the company for an occasional weekend to play minor roles.

After the coming of total film unionization in wartime, such a project could never happen again, but it left Mason with a residual affection for private movie-making and the control it gave him, one for which he always yearned futilely during major studio productions in the years to come. *I Met A Murderer* (this more intriguing title than *Deadwater* was given to Pamela by the actress Leonora Corbett at a party soon after the shooting finally wound up in the autumn of 1938) is the kind of film that could best be called 'interesting': it has a grainy sort of integrity, and for the first time on camera Mason does seem to have a commanding control and intensity, as though for once he was not vaguely ashamed to be caught acting for a living.

It was, as so often, the critic James Agee who was later in *The Nation* to express most clearly the virtues and vices of the picture: 'Though it tries too hard for its own artistic good (and often with remarkable smoothness) to look "professional", *I Met A Murderer* is streaked with enough amateurishness to pretty well guarantee its commercial failure. There are some downright poor things in it, but this is one of the fairly few movies I have seen in years where it was clear that the makers knew and cared, and in general had lively and sensible ideas about how each shot should follow the next, and what in the way of emotion, atmosphere, observation and psychological weight and progression each shot and each group of shots should contain. I also thought it graceful, gallant, resourceful and in every way satisfying and encouraging in its broken-field run through the problems of cost and production. It is better and more enjoyable than most studio pictures.'

As far as Mason was concerned, 'this was my first really important picture, a breakthrough of some description because it was an interesting project'. One, however, that barely made it out of the Buckinghamshire cottage that the Kellinos were still sharing with Mason, and around which much of the film was made. When it was completed and cut, still without any studio backing or interest of any kind, Pamela took it to her family who were then in charge of distribution at Gaumont-British, and therefore in charge also of about half the cinemas in Britain.

The five brothers (Pamela's father and four uncles) who ran the business in those pre-Rank days took one look at the film and decided that, family ties or none, they wanted nothing to do with it since this was patently a home-made and probably uncommercial picture. Their instant refusal to tolerate it not only enraged Pamela, but left James with a residual loathing for the British film distribution

45

network which was to erupt a few years later into a long and damaging battle with the Rank Organisation. It also left *I Met A Murderer* for almost two years without any distribution at all at home or abroad, since other exhibitors naturally enough figured that if Pamela's own family weren't prepared to screen it in their cinemas, it must indeed be a dead loser.

In the meantime, James remained unemployed and in considerable career trouble: *I Met A Murderer* had occupied him unpaid for almost the whole of 1938, and though it had undoubtedly been a rewarding intellectual and production experience, it had taken him virtually out of circulation and there now seemed to be no professional demands of any kind for his services. Apart from one brief return to his ever-faithful Dublin Gate at the end of November to play Lord Byron in a James Laver stage adaptation of the poet's life – one so apparently unmemorable that even Mason failed to recall it in his own memoirs – he was now chronically out of work, and worried even about his recent decision to rent a small flat in Marylebone High Street to which he could retreat with several of his beloved cats whenever life with the Kellinos got more than usually strained.

At this uneasy point in his career, he started a lifelong friendship, though never an affair, with the concert singer and restaurant owner Diana de Rosso, who was also a half-sister of Pamela's:

'I think that apart from his second wife, Clarissa, I probably got to know James as well as anyone ever could. I often think that Pamela hardly knew him at all. I used to tell him that he was totally cardboard, because he never showed anger or passion of any kind. That dark and stormy-looking man wasn't really dark or stormy at all: he was nervous, diffident, constantly in doubt about his own work and his own life. Everything always had to be examined by him, taken apart and looked at over and over again. He was a great craftsman, highly emotional, addicted to the silent films of Buster Keaton, but totally hung over from his own very English schooldays, where he was treated to all the ritual humiliations of Marlborough. His own very proper upbringing, with the nanny and the seaside holidays, had left him as what the French called *un solitaire*, terribly ill-at-ease, always nervous. With Pam she was always the one who did the talking. He was one of the most withdrawn men I've ever met, but I loved him very much.'

Diana and Pamela were the daughters of different fathers, as Diana explains, 'I was the cause of the Ostrers' divorce, because he knew I couldn't possibly be his daughter. But Pamela and I grew up reasonably closely and I remember hearing about this charming young actor whom she had met. The next thing I remember was Roy complaining to our mother that James was always in their home, this very good-looking, rather shy young man. One gathered that he was an admirer of Pam's. Later Roy began to treat James like a brother, and I think in the end those two men were as great and constant friends as any two men could ever be. Roy may have resented James at first, but he was very easy-going and really rather proud that Pamela attracted so much attention. I think he thought it was a feather in his cap that other men wanted her, and he really was devoted to James even years after the divorce.

'Our mother used to worry a bit about whether James was really breaking up Pamela's marriage, because he did seem to be always there like a sort of barnacle, but I don't remember any real dramas or quarrels. All three of them used to come over to tea with us in the country and one just got accustomed to them being together.

'Roy occasionally used to rebel and throw James out of the house, and I remember James looking rather surprised and aggrieved at this, but then after a day or two Pam would be on the phone and he'd be back.'

Meanwhile James's career was now about to be rescued from its doldrums, for the second time, by another faithful and lifelong friend, Al Parker.

11

*'My own war record maintained a consistently low rating:
I knew I had a sense of responsibility, but found little trace
of anything that could be described as a sense of duty.'*

IN THE TWO years after James left him to make *Mill on the Floss*,
Al Parker had made a few more quota quickies and then reckoned
that once again his career was in need of the kind of revival he had
given it before by quitting Hollywood for London after the halcyon
years with Fairbanks. This time, he decided, it would be a slight
shift of profession, and by early 1939 he had set up as an actors'
agent, though initially without any clients. This was the moment
when Parker decided to bury the hatchet with Mason and invite him
to join the agency, an offer which in the absence of any others Mason
found impossible to refuse. Al Parker was to remain his agent for
the rest of his life, and on Parker's death it was his widow Maggie
who took over for the latter part of James's career.

But even Parker, whose faith in Mason's future stardom remained
as undimmed as it had been on the day of their first quota-quickie
meeting, was unable to do much about the doldrums into which
James's career had sunk with the non-release of *I Met A Murderer*.
He did get him into one shortlived stage thriller (*Sixth Floor*) at the
St James's in May 1939, but beyond that it was in some desperation
that both men turned away from the cinema and the theatre towards
a new and untried medium, then largely populated by those whose
careers were in trouble elsewhere: television.

Through most of 1939, until the outbreak of war in September, James worked in half a dozen plays transmitted live from Alexandra Palace by the BBC, among them Molière's *The Miser*, Priestley's *Bees on the Boatdeck*, Johnston's *Moon in the Yellow River* and Maugham's *The Circle*, which was actually in rehearsal when war was declared. Live television delighted him, if only because he was already wary of repeating the same performance night after night on stage, even if his luck should ever change and a long run come his way. At Alexandra Palace, as in the early repertory days around England and Ireland and again just after the war when at another troubled time he was to take regularly to live radio in New York, he seemed to find a kind of cavalier friendship and entertainment that somehow eluded him on the more familiar territory of movie studios.

But the coming of the war itself served to focus people's minds miraculously on situations that had previously been allowed to drift along in a haze of private and professional uncertainty. *I Met A Murderer* was at last given a limited screening at the Marble Arch Pavilion, soon ended by the coming of war, whereupon the distributors took the negative to America, lost it in mid-Atlantic during a submarine attack, later found another copy and gave that a partial release after considerable transatlantic legal squabbling. But by now the director-producer Roy Kellino no longer found it tolerable to stay under the same roof as his wife and James; he therefore left home, shortly to file for divorce citing Mason.

James, meanwhile, was due for appearance in another early-wartime courtroom of a different kind: one of the things that he shared with Pamela was a strong sense of pacifism, a belief that all wars were wrong and that it was therefore totally wrong to encourage them by joining up. At just the moment when his two elder brothers were joining the Army and the Navy, James applied for a tribunal hearing as a conscientious objector. Relations with his family, which had deteriorated considerably when they discovered he was living with a married woman, now reached an all-time low, as Rex recalls:

'Pamela was a very striking and intelligent woman who always seemed to be managing James, though I think the pacifism was very deep in him. My parents were appalled at having a son who suddenly decided not to do his bit for the country; for eight years we none of us saw him, and there's no doubt that it caused a real rift within the family. We still went to see his films, though at that time I never thought he was very good in them. Eventually he came back to us, desperately embarrassed by the split, and gradually we got together again: but it did take a very long time for us all to forget what had happened.'

There are, of course, a number of ways in which James's decision to become a conscientious objector can be viewed with the wisdom of hindsight. It could have been the act of a coward, or of a professional opportunist who saw a chance to acquire, while others were at war, the kind of leading roles which he had never achieved in peacetime. On the other hand it could have been an act of deep personal courage, performed out of moral conviction and regardless of the consequences, which at that time could have been severe.

True, James did not at this point have a wide public following and his decision not to fight did not attract headlines of stunned horror; but within the profession it was much discussed, and certainly his action lost him one major movie role when Noël Coward refused to cast him for *In Which We Serve* since he had declined a uniform in real life. Others were more tolerant, and ironically Mason was encouraged very early in the war to tour army camps for ENSA (the British military entertainment service) with a trio of quite remarkably unsuccessful dramas: indeed so few soldiers turned out to watch them that Mason and his co-star Raymond Lovell took to inviting those that had around to the nearest pub, rather than making them sit through the rest of their not very inspired performances.

Mason spent much of 1940 in a kind of limbo, waiting for things to happen that now seemed more than ever outside his control: Kellino had to get his divorce; the tribunal had to rule on his conscientious objection; some sort of decision had to be made about his future with Pamela; and meanwhile there was a war on, and he still had some sort of career to re-activate.

This last, at least, looked as though it might be possible when Gaby Pascal, alongside Korda the other great immigrant movie mogul of the Thirties and Forties, approached him early in the year with the offer of Adolphus Cusins in the *Major Barbara* he was about to start shooting with Wendy Hiller and Robert Morley. James saw at once that this was precisely the kind of distinguished leading role for which he had been waiting too long, and tested extensively before being told by Pascal that, alas, the role had gone instead to Andrew Osborn.

Needing to make some money elsewhere, he and Pamela took to the road in a tour of A. J. Cronin's *Jupiter Laughs,* a desultory little drama which folded rapidly as the provincial air raids grew worse. They both then retreated to a rented cottage near Taplow, where Pamela turned back to her life as a novelist. By now it seems to have been accepted that they would eventually marry, once Kellino got his divorce, but as the producer and screenwriter Edward Dryhurst noted, theirs had always been a curious design for living:

'During the planning of *I Met A Murderer* I once arrived at their London flat to be greeted by Pamela and Roy, and when we went into the lounge I saw that Jimmy Mason was stretched out on a couch immersed in a book. To the best of my recollection he did not participate in the ensuing discussion [about the film] between Roy, Pamela and myself, which would have been entirely in character for there were times when James went into his shell. From my experience of him he was a man of moods; one day he could be a lively and entertaining conversationalist, the next silent and uptight. But he was likable for all that ... As filming progressed it became all too evident that the mutual attraction of our leading man and lady was going beyond the demands of the script, but Roy seemed unperturbed; by now he was perhaps resigned to the inevitable ... Once I asked him that he was going to do about it and he sighed. "I made him hop it the other evening, but the bugger was back in the morning."'

Now, however, the relationship had simply become that of a couple awaiting a divorce, and James seemed if anything more concerned with his appearance in Maidenhead before a conscientious-objection tribunal. His application was rejected and he was directed to do non-combatant service, without ever being told what this might entail. In the event he was soon transferred to 'reserved' status, and allowed, like many actors, to stay out of uniform on the grounds that filming was war work of national importance, so long as there was a 'recognisable' demand for his services.

And this there luckily soon turned out to be. First of all Gaby Pascal reappeared with the news that Andrew Osborn was no longer playing Cusins in *Major Barbara,* and that the part was therefore his. By this time Mason had learned not to put over-excessive faith in the promises of Pascal: four days later, he opened a paper to read that Rex Harrison had started shooting on the film. Instead he went into yet another doomed regional tour, this one with Frances Day, of a comedy called *Divorce for Christobel*. Its jokes about adultery and co-respondents struck Mason as a little close to home, especially as Pamela and James had been obliged to sit up together in bed one morning so that a maid could give due evidence of marital infidelity.

Having no idea whether he might soon be sent off to some factory or farm as a 'non-combatant', Mason decided to learn at least a little about the land, so he set up a thriving poultry farm in Beaconsfield. Ronald Gow and Wendy Hiller remember some excellent wartime eggs personally delivered around the district by James on a bicycle. Clearly eggs were not going to provide him with a living, however, and as there was only a very little money coming in from Pamela's writing it was with a kind of relief that he accepted an offer to get in a couple of low-budget thrillers then being made by Pathé out at Welwyn Garden City. Though not exactly quota quickies, *This Man is Dangerous* and *The Night Has Eyes* were certainly not in the class of films to which James had hoped that either Korda or Pascal or his own production efforts on *I Met A Murderer* would promote him. On the other hand, they were regular work, and they came at a time when he was in no personal or professional position to turn that down.

12

'At the press showing of The Man in Grey *I found myself next to the critic C. A. Lejeune. "This," she said "is an occasion well worth celebrating: the birth of a great new English film star – Stewart Granger".'*

IN FEBRUARY 1941, just after the shooting of *This Man is Dangerous* (in which Mason was typecast as a detective in search of a millionaire's missing daughter), he and Pamela were quietly married in an Amersham registry office. James then immediately returned to work on *The Night Has Eyes* (this time playing a composer living as a recluse on Dartmoor, terrified that he might be a homicidal maniac), and doubled that with a brief West End run in a revival of *Jupiter Laughs* in which he had toured during the previous year.

True to his usual theatrical luck, this fell like a bag of wet sand onto the stage of the New Theatre, and has the minor distinction of constituting his last ever West End appearance: critics felt that A. J. Cronin's first original play was a trifle melodramatic, but as Mason memorably told a backstage interviewer at the time: 'If an author wants to blow up his heroine in a laboratory explosion, why not? And why shouldn't God and the purposes of Science be discussed on the stage?'

Audiences seeking respite from the Blitz were in search of something lighter, and though *Jupiter Laughs* soon closed it did at least afford Mason (who had doubled as director) a useful connection with Cronin which led almost immediately to *Hatter's Castle*, the first notable movie in which he was to have a sizable role.

53

Here he was in good company: Robert Newton, Deborah Kerr and Emlyn Williams ensured a level of performance rather higher than Mason had come to expect of his co-stars in the B-to-Z thrillers which had occupied most of his screen time. Though Dilys Powell reckoned that *Hatter's Castle* was still no more than prime ham, 'an extremely competent piece of work', it is important in the Mason story for two reasons. First, its popular success seemed to launch him on a quite remarkable period of screen activity: in the remaining four years of the war he was to make no less than a dozen pictures, all improved considerably in budgets and ambition from the quickies of his immediate past. And secondly, in the comparatively unrewarding role of the decent local doctor loved by Deborah Kerr, the tyrannical Hatter's daughter, he began to perfect the brooding sexiness which was soon to give him his wartime stardom.

As soon as it was completed, James went straight into *Alibi*, playing not altogether convincingly the role of a young Parisian policeman, one created a few years earlier by Louis Jouvet in the original Eric von Stroheim version. It was a curious little nightclub murder mystery, mainly notable now for the fact that Mason was able to demand co-star billing with Margaret Lockwood and Hugh Sinclair. 'A good looker', thought the *Sunday Express*, 'Mason has a nice style of his own.' That led on to *Secret Mission*, his first war film and one in which he and Hugh Williams were cast as a couple of Anglo-French secret agents out to discover hidden Nazi fortifications in occupied France.

Then he played the tough fire-station commander in *The Bells Go Down*, which was (he rather sadly noted) his only ever job in an Ealing picture, and not an especially distinguished one at that. But his last film of 1942, indeed his last before achieving genuine personal stardom early in the following year, was a cut above the rest: *Thunder Rock*.

'During the shooting of *Thunder Rock*,' recalls the writer and producer Vivian Cox, 'I was staying at Denham near my old friend and school housemaster Michael Redgrave, and visiting him on the set I got to know James. We used to lunch together and engage in long debates about his pacifism. I wondered whether it was just a device to get work at a time when others were away and unavailable, but I came to the conclusion that he was totally sincere. Redgrave was always a shadow over James. They had been together as students

54

at Cambridge, and later when Michael decided to be a schoolmaster there is no doubt that James was very relieved. But then Redgrave did come into the business, and from then on I think James knew that Michael would always get the best of the work in the theatre. They never played together again after *Thunder Rock*, but whereas Michael was perfectly happy to watch James becoming a film star, I think James was always rather envious of the stage distinction which Redgrave achieved and he somehow never did.

'Later, when James occasionally came back from Hollywood, I would see him around the studios, first of all with Pamela and then on his own. He was a very feline man, but totally honest about his professional life, which he always viewed with a kind of sadness, as though he'd have much preferred to be Redgrave if fate had worked out that way. He was a loyal man, shy and desperate to avoid any confrontation in public or private. For years afterwards we maintained a kind of correspondence, and towards the end of his life he appeared in the Royal Film Performances I organized in Leicester Square, always worrying terribly about his stage presence. I think he found it very nerve-racking.'

Thunder Rock was the screen version of Robert Ardrey's classic play about the British writer (Michael Redgrave on stage and screen) who goes to a lonely Lake Michigan lighthouse to escape a wartime civilization of which he despairs, only there to be faced with the ghosts who are in a sense his own conscience. Mason played the comparatively brief role of the American friend who tries to bring Redgrave back into the real world. The film was thought by the *Manchester Guardian* to be 'the most intelligent ever produced in Britain, and more interesting technically than anything since *Citizen Kane*'.

It did not, however, do for Mason anything like as much good as his next picture, a costumed hunk of what James Agate was to call 'bosh and tosh' but one which nonetheless established him in the view of the *Motion Picture Herald* as England's most popular screen actor.

The history of *The Man in Grey* is a curious one. A Regency novel by Lady Eleanor Smith about a sadistic aristocrat, it had lain gathering dust on library shelves until the writer and producer R. J. Minney brought it to the attention of James's in-laws the Ostrers, who were by now working within the J. Arthur Rank Organization.

There it was decided that, in the words of a later *Time* magazine critic, *The Man in Grey* had everything: 'A heavily romantic, sugary swashbuckler containing all the time-tested materials: a gypsy fortune-teller, a scowling and black-browed villain, a gushing diary kept by a doe-eyed girl named Clarissa who munches candied violets, a wavy-haired hero with beautifully strong teeth, and a fire-breathing adventuress who dotes on discord and low-cut gowns.'

Under the familiar logo of Gainsborough Studios, a subsidiary of Rank, Minney and the Ostrers began to pull a production together: Margaret Kennedy (of the *Constant Nymph*), and the director Leslie Arliss (with whom Mason had already squabbled during *The Night Has Eyes*), were commissioned to come up with a screenplay memorable for lines like 'Without you the day is too long'; 'I don't think I can bear this', and 'You address the last of the Rohans'. Although Robert Donat briskly declined to play the hero, he did at least recommend a young man with whom he had been at the Old Vic called Stewart Granger. For the 'good' and 'bad' women Phyllis Calvert and Margaret Lockwood were cast – the start of a long partnership in such roles – and that left just the problem of finding the evil, aristocratic Marquis of Rohan.

The first thought here had been Eric Portman, but when he declined shortly before filming was due to start the Ostrers turned in some desperation to their Pamela's new husband who, hating every page of the script but encouraged by Al Parker to believe that this could be a big moneymaker, agreed to sneer his way through the rubbish. Indeed, so keen was James to get it that he even broke the rule of a lifetime and signed with Rank for a five-picture contract, a decision he regretted almost before the ink was dry on the paper.

As a result, he played *The Man in Grey* in a state of ill-concealed fury: he hated the part, the script, the film, and still more the prospect of four more like it, however profitable they might turn out to be. He also hated being at the beck and call of any producer or director for more than about ten weeks, let alone enslaved for months if not years to a studio still largely run by the hated in-laws who had been so unhelpful over *I Met a Murderer*. And he had already established on a previous picture that he hated the director: indeed this time he actually once hit him, rather than obey some mindless instruction.

But it was, of course, precisely that sustained, seething anger which made his performance as Lord Rohan so memorable. 'Only my permanent aggravation on the set', said James later, 'gave the character colour and made it some sort of a memorable thing.' So memorable, in fact, that when the picture opened in New York one local critic announced that 'swaggering through the title role, sneering like Laughton, barking like Gable and frowning like Laurence Olivier on a dark night, Mason is likely to pick up many a feminine fan'.

So after nineteen films, and thirteen years as an actor, at the age of thirty-five Mason had become an international movie star in, all too typically, a swashbuckler that he could never bring himself to watch, let alone talk about in any but the most depressed and dismissive terms. And like him, but rather more happily and enthusiastically, Gainsborough realized at once what they had stumbled into with *The Man in Grey*: not just one Regency costume parade, but a potential sequence of melodramas with Granger and Calvert as the goodies and Mason and Lockwood as the baddies, one which would do for wartime audiences and box-office attendance what *Dynasty* and *Dallas* were to do for television ratings forty years later.

At first James was allowed a brief escape into pictures that had been lined up before the Rank contract: the first of these three war movies was *They Met in the Dark,* hotly followed by *Candlelight in Algeria* and *Hotel Reserve.* Each was concerned to some degree with espionage and enemy agents in occupied territory, and it was not really surprising that James should have given virtually the same performance in all three. He then returned to the dreaded Gainsborough melodramas.

Though the catchline 'mean, moody and magnificent' had already been appropriated by Hollywood for one of its female stars, it was in precisely those terms that the Rank Organization now went about the selling of Mason at home and abroad. From being an interesting, intellectual player at his best in such poetic dramas as *Thunder Rock,* he had suddenly become the infinitely more accessible and marketable 'man you love to hate'.

It is perhaps to Mason's credit that he at once saw the dangers in allowing himself to end up as the Home Counties answer to Eric von Stroheim. Torn between a desire to make a decent living for Pamela and the family they intended to have, and the hope that he might still be allowed to make pictures that he himself could bear to watch, Mason went through these three Rank years in a state of clenched fury which soon enough got him the label of 'difficult'. It wasn't that he was ever unprofessional: lines were learned, cues were given, marks were hit and costume or wig fittings, like premieres, were regularly attended. On screen he gave value for money, but off-screen he made so abundantly clear the extent to which he despised not only the pictures they were making but the Rank Organization in its every aspect that he came fairly low on in-studio popularity polls. The truth was simple enough: he hated being in pictures he couldn't control, and disliked still more being in pictures that he found so far beneath his own intelligence and critical judgement as to be almost out of sight.

Second to *The Man in Grey* was *Fanny By Gaslight*, with James as the evil Lord Manderstoke instead of the evil Lord Rohan, this time being unspeakable not to Phyllis Calvert as Clarissa Rohan but to Phyllis Calvert as Fanny Hopwood, who was duly saved from him not by Stewart Granger as Peter Rokeby but by Stewart Granger as Harry Somerford. True, this time they had Jean Kent rather than Margaret Lockwood giving her wicked lady, but in all other respects *Fanny By Gaslight* was *The Man in Grey* moved from Regency to Victorian times. 'Mr Mason is horrid,' thought C. A. Lejeune, and that in the circumstances was praise indeed.

For Stewart Granger, equally appalled by his Gainsborough surroundings but junior to Mason and less inclined at that point to show his general displeasure, this second period costume picture was mainly notable for the picnics that James used to bring onto the set. 'He always arrived with baskets of goodies,' Granger recalled. 'Eggs, tinned salmon, tinned sardines, butter, chocolate, all very scarce in those days. He was married to my boss's niece, Pamela Ostrer, who was not exactly penniless ... I had neither the contacts nor the money for these delicacies, and James would share them with his constantly starving friend Granger: lunch was always a high spot in my working day with him.'

For Phyllis Calvert, who was to appear in four of these Gainsborough costume pictures with James, 'the curious thing about him was that he always remained so secretive and solitary. From the audience I'd already fallen in love with him in bad B pictures, and the first thing I noticed on the set was that whenever Pamela appeared he would visibly brighten, as though she'd shone a light on him. Both of them seemed very concerned about the war, and of course James was a pacifist, though that didn't prevent him hitting one of our directors, Leslie Arliss, thereby giving birth to the phrase "Arlissing about".

'We all knew that he had been living with Pamela and her first husband, but in those days nobody liked to ask too much about it, and there was never any way of breaking through that intellectual, impersonal, academic reserve. I think he was a wonderful, lonely actor who longed to be taken more seriously than he ever was at Gainsborough.'

13

'My experience with producers made me regard them all as my natural enemies.'

AFTER TWO SWAGGERING historical soap-operatic villains, and on the way to the one that would crown them all, Mason managed to convince his masters at Rank that even he deserved time off for good behaviour, and preferably in a picture that didn't fit the routine format quite so relentlessly. The film he had in mind was *A Place of One's Own,* Osbert Sitwell's elegant Victorian ghost story of spirits from beyond the grave, which, unusually, allowed him to age by about thirty years in order to play the retired Mr Smedhurst, baffled owner of the haunted house. Mason fought long and hard for this role in an attempt to escape the 'man you love to hate' typecasting, and was rewarded by a major commercial flop. The public which had now put him ahead of Ronald Colman in movie-magazine popularity charts was making it clear that they wanted Mason as a villain, and preferably in period, rather than Mason as character actor of considerable versatility. It was a box-office demand which James spent much of the rest of his life, and usually in exile, fighting against; but that was a battle he really only won after another thirty years and fifty pictures.

In the meantime, faced with the flop of *A Place of One's Own,* Gainsborough rapidly abandoned plans to cast him as Pierre Laval, the Vichy government's Prime Minister, in a film (never made) about the fall of France, and instead put him straight into *They Were Sisters* where, apparently suffering from a succession of hangovers, he was allowed to snarl so continuously at faithful wife Dulcie Gray that she finally threw herself under a car, thereby confirming his villainous reputation to the satisfaction of Odeon audiences across the country.

But the more successful he became in villainy, the more irritable and withdrawn James became about his work: by the end of 1945 polls were showing that for the previous year he and David Niven, who had made no top ten appearances in the box-office charts before, were in the first two positions nationwide, followed by George Formby, Eric Portman, Laurence Olivier, Margaret Lockwood, Robert Donat, Phyllis Calvert, Anna Neagle and Robert Newton on home screens. Of this list only Niven, Donat and Olivier had made any American impact, but there was no doubt, thought the editors of the *Motion Picture Herald*, that 'it's a safe assumption Mr Mason will be Hollywood-bound in due course: there is a warm earnestness to his acting and even a mellow romantic air which, when allowed to overcome the villainy, commends itself to audiences of every sort'.

Meanwhile it was back to Gainsborough villainy, though mercifully for the last time. *The Wicked Lady*, 'a sombre picture masquerading as an eighteenth-century romp' in the view of one critic, cast Mason again opposite Lockwood 'in their usual roles of brutal heart-throb and lively wench, without much concern for the fact that its plot demands Lockwood to be a lady of quality and Mason a highwayman with a code of honour'. Mason in fact appears to be sleep-walking through much of the action, and in later years recalled only a clause in his contract whereby, because his part was so much smaller than Lockwood's, none of his scenes could be cut without his prior consent. Surprisingly, he fought for the retention of all of them, and *Time* magazine did acknowledge his 'determined efforts to rise above the handicaps of uninspired direction, flat photography and a deadweight of costumes'. The *Observer* reckoned it 'an odd mix of hot passion and cold suet pudding', though *The Times* thought that James managed well enough as 'Macheath without the songs, bringing a fine swagger of indifference and bravado'. Simon Harcourt-Smith for *Tribune* remained less than wholly won over:

'There exists, of course, no reason why J. Arthur Rank should not sanction the inflicting on us of whatever dowdy fancy-dress inanity he will. Lines that issue from a mouth imprisoned between a cotton-wool wig and a machine-made lace cravat appear to please the average audience where they would be intolerable in modern melodrama. And certainly *The Wicked Lady* is infused with a nonsense of period so authentically Hollywood that it should almost qualify for one of those American releases that must, we gather, be the yardstick of excellence ... But *The Wicked Lady* arouses in me a nausea out of all proportion to the subject. Perhaps I should not cavil at this complete misunderstanding of Restoration England, the tatty Merry-English-Roadhouse atmosphere with the bowls of "daffies" on gate-legged tables and the ladylike carousings of pretty Miss Lockwood, with a James Mason so embarrassed and yet so competent that he arouses at once both admiration and sympathy.'

Critics' cavils notwithstanding, *The Wicked Lady* became the runaway box-office success of 1945. James still owed Gainsborough at least one more film, but his own desire to get back to theatre led to a couple of ENSA and American Red Cross tours, during one of which Mason's increasing disaffection with the Rank Organization first came to public attention.

Out of a lingering desire to be taken more seriously than his costumed caperings would allow, and also out of sheer boredom with the work in hand, James had taken to some occasional journalism; early in 1945, he published in a movie magazine a querulous but generally unobjectionable column pointing out that the more closely you got involved in the day-to-day making of Gainsborough pictures, the less appealing they were.

'It is true certainly that I find precious little glamour in British pictures ... I know that everyone concerned in the making of the picture hated his work, and the only reason the darned thing was made at all is that, someone way back having paid £10,000 for the story and a further £20,000 on shooting long shots and back-projection plates, the head of the company decided that as a plain statement of loss this sum would look rather ugly on the books and the shareholders might then ask embarrassing questions. I know that the male star whom the publicity department is taking such pains to bolster is only playing the part because everyone else they approached threw the script back in their faces. I know that the director was sacked halfway through because he quarrelled with the leading lady, and that the scenario editor was prevailed upon to go through the motions of directing the rest of the picture. I know that one of the featured actors had to be photographed only from the waist up because he had fallen out of a window in a drunken stupor and broken his leg. I know that a lawsuit is pending because someone on the cutting-room staff claims to have thought of the title ... Indeed it would be a glum outlook for me if there were not still a Hollywood. And I do love my Hollywood ...'.

Insofar as James ever wrote a death threat to his English career and a one-way ticket to America, this was it.

14

'The Seventh Veil was quite simply the most successful film I ever made, and the welcome mat was then spread all over Hollywood.'

IRONICALLY, AT THE time he wrote his controversial article, Mason had never visited America and had no intention of doing so; his piece was merely a groan of studio boredom, ended by the vague acknowledgement that things looked a lot more exciting over in California for those who had managed to get there in easier, pre-war times. But at a moment when, with the coming end to the war, British studios were attempting to get back on their feet and to fight off the continuing American invasion of local cinema screens, James's writing seemed like the act of a traitor. Those who had somehow managed, in studios and cinemas alike, not to get too worried about his pacifism, now got extremely alarmed about his apparent treachery.

The director Anthony Asquith, who had worked with Mason on *Fanny By Gaslight* and who also happened to be chairman of the Association of Cinema Technicians, issued a public rebuttal of Mason's article almost as soon as it hit the streets: 'We think it a little unfortunate that someone of your standing who, we are sure you would admit, owes something to the efforts of British technicians should give such an unfair and misleading impression of the British film industry. Your article might do great harm in America, especially now when we are doing our utmost, and not without success, to get our films shown there. We have all, of course, had unfortunate experiences during our film work, but we cannot imagine anywhere in the world where this would not be true and to imply that such conditions are the general rule is not only impolitic but ungrateful. Far from being ashamed of the present British film industry, you will find that the majority of our technicians have been proud to work on films made in this country during the war and they would be quite prepared to set them against the American 'glamour' you mention. No doubt you intended your article as a joke; but its effects might be serious, and we can only hope that when you wrote it you were not conscious of the harm it might do to British films and yourself.'

Quite apart from the vague threat (presumably of future unemployment) contained in its last words, Asquith's reprimand was a prime example of the kind of authoritarian humourlessness and pomposity that Mason found so objectionable within the Rank Organisation in particular and the British film industry in general. In professional career terms, by early 1945 James was really only waiting for an end to his English career; at the height of his Gainsborough fame he had made two deeply disquieting calculations. One was that even in a good year, the British film industry could expect at most six good movies (one Reed, one Asquith, one David Lean, one Powell and Pressburger, one Launder and Gilliatt and one 'fluke' hit), and the second was that his chances of getting into even any one of them would usually depend on the unavailability of Laurence Olivier, Trevor Howard, Rex Harrison or Michael Redgrave, always assuming both Niven and Richard Greene went back to Hollywood after the fighting.

In short, Mason reckoned his future was bleak in the extreme: his Gainsborough hits had still not had time to elicit any offers from California, and all he knew was that he couldn't face making any more of them anyway. So what was he to do?

The ENSA army-camp touring only served to remind him that he no longer much cared for the prospect of a stage life, and it took just one more of his articles (characteristically entitled 'I Hate Producers') to convince Gainsborough that there would be little point in holding Mason to the remnants of his contract, especially as they had no very suitable script in the pipeline.

If Mason had simply wanted to do himself out of a job, or at any rate escape a tedious contract, then his journalism had proved singularly effective; but he did now have to start thinking about where else to find work. It was at this point that he came to the attention of precisely the kind of director he was looking for. Michael Powell recalled: 'This dark young god had always been bitter about the way his contemporaries and rivals all got their feet in the door ahead of him, especially as he longed to play the great parts and was physically and mentally equipped to do so. He had a voice and a bearing second to none, and his marriage to Pamela had certainly helped his career, for she was clever and active as a wasp ... A few years before his death, Nigel Balchin described to me his first sight of James Mason when they were both undergraduates ... it was down at the boats, and Nigel described a tall, black-haired, magnificently built young man in white rowing shorts and a singlet which modelled the graceful shape of his muscular limbs. Nigel was a master of words and phrases, and in that moment I saw that wonderful young man exactly as Nigel had seen him on that sunshiny morning.'

Powell wanted Mason to play the lead opposite Wendy Hiller in *I Know Where I'm Going*, but negotiations proved impossible. 'They were suspicious and I was enigmatic,' recalled Powell of his first meeting with Pamela and James. 'Three more aggressive personalities had surely never met ... they pelted me with questions about how I proposed to do this and that, and my answers became shorter and shorter as such questions always irk me: I loved the movies and had been in them long enough to know that everything can be done.'

All the same, it was finally agreed that Mason would take the role of the young naval lieutenant, at any rate until Powell and Emeric Pressburger went off to Mull to start scouting for locations and announced that the cast and crew would be living far from any town or hotel in base-camp conditions on the island. Powell thereupon received a curt telegram from James announcing that he was too old for such boy-scouting, and would have to withdraw unless first-class hotel accommodation could be provided. It couldn't.

The role went to Roger Livesey, who seemed less concerned about off-camera living arrangements during the shoot, but this proved in its own way a happy escape for Mason, since it left him free for the next offer that came along. The director Sydney Box and his wife Muriel had, during the last year of the war, been commissioned to make a documentary about the use of hypnosis in curing shell-shocked soldiers. It was Muriel who saw in this something more than a documentary: what if the hypnosis were to be performed on a concert painist? The script they started to work on was called *The Seventh Veil*.

Once again Mason was being asked to take on a role which would require him to strike a woman, in this case Ann Todd at the keyboard: 'If you will not play for me, then you will play for no one.' On the other hand, even he could see that the circumstances here were vastly more promising than those surrounding the Gainsborough farragos of his recent past. The script, by Muriel and Sydney Box, was virtually the first British attempt to take psychiatry seriously on the screen, and as such it led to regular work for Herbert Lom as the sympathetic shrink as well as satisfying Mason's intellectual curiosity in a way that precious few screenplays had ever managed to in the past. For that reason *The Seventh Veil* was, in Mason's own view, one of his rare 'adult' movies, and it led to an on and off-screen affair of considerable passion, as Ann Todd recalls:

'I suppose you could say that our friendship really began on the set of *The Seventh Veil*. He was already a very big star because of the Gainsborough costume pictures and I was very nervous of him, which I suppose was what our film relationship was all about. But his sudden laughter and a curious kind of need to be loved made him really terribly attractive. We never settled down together, both of us always seemed to be married to other people and usually the wrong people, but looking back on it now I don't think I've ever been as close to anyone in my life as I was to James, and we do seem to have achieved something together in that one film which lives on in people's memories.'

Few critics disagreed: made in only ten weeks on a very tight budget of £100,000, with the concert pianist Eileen Joyce playing offscreen for Miss Todd, it was hailed alongside the contemporary American *The Lost Weekend* (about alcoholism) as a welcome sign of the 'growing up' of the cinema, and of its new-found ability to tackle mature and difficult themes.

As Ann Todd later noted, 'It was the film that had everything – a bit of *Pygmalion*, a bit of *Trilby* and a bit of *Cinderella*. Apart from all that it's an intriguing psychological drama and was one of the first films to have a hero who was cruel. Most male stars up to then had been honest, kind, upstanding, good-looking men that the female star was supposed to feel safe and secure with for the rest of her life when they finally got together at the end of the film. Not so with our smash hit. The men saw me as a victim and the women thrilled to Mason's power and cruelty, as women have thrilled to this since the world began, however much they deny it . . . it's interesting, too, that the film has a lot of sex in it, although there are no love scenes between Mason and me; in fact he never touches me throughout the film.'

Unless of course you count him hitting her across the fingers at the keyboard, for which Ann Todd received a quarter of a million pounds, that being the value of the contract Rank now offered her. As for James, he was still regarded as contractually untouchable because of his widely published attacks on the studio, but he was at least now established for the first time in modern dress as a powerful box-office prospect, a postwar Svengali with his own hypnotically intense screen presence. Not surprisingly, he began to think about Hollywood at precisely the moment when it was beginning to think about him.

15

'Odd Man Out was a great film and perhaps Carol Reed's best: certainly it was mine.'

JAMES MASON HAD, as usual, not been the first choice for the piano tutor in *The Seventh Veil*: that honour belonged to the still more sinister Francis L. Sullivan, who got caught up in the over-running of the epic Vivien Leigh *Caesar and Cleopatra*. But Mason's performance in it was undoubtedly what first established the film's huge critical and popular success, as well as his own new-found credibility as a leading man fit not only to horsewhip Margaret Lockwood but to play vastly more impressive and thoughtful scripts. The problem for him now was simply how to build on that success, given that his own recalcitrance and horror of the British studios had effectively divorced him from any support system. He was a temperamental freelance in a film world still almost entirely peopled by long-term contract artists.

But Sydney Box, himself an independent who had only recently escaped the clutches of Denham to form his own production unit, quickly suggested that James might like to come up with a project of his own, which was of course precisely the invitation for which he and Pamela had been waiting since their collaboration on *I Met A Murderer* seven years previously. In fact they even had a project already in mind, a life of the Brontë family written by Pamela in which James would star as the brooding Branwell, but as they went into pre-production they found that Hollywood already had a Brontë story on general release in America.

Rapidly changing their plans, they turned instead to another psychological thriller called *The Upturned Glass* in which James (who co-produced with Sydney Box) played a brilliant young surgeon driven to murder and insanity by Pamela (who had also co-written the script and was making her first screen appearance since a fleeting performance as, curiously, James's daughter in *They Were Sisters*), playing his femme fatale. 'Mr Mason is now getting very adept at tense romantic doom,' thought the *New Statesman*, while James himself reckoned: 'We did rather well considering that the whole thing was a spur-of-the-moment operation designed to take advantage of the freak success of *The Seventh Veil*. It was an important moment for Betty Box, Sydney's sister, who was also one of the producers: she sailed with her tide and became the most sensible and hardworking producer in the British industry, where she remained one of its few survivors. I consciously missed my tide and set off, but without regrets, to a programme of daft adventure in the United States.'

The attraction of California was obvious. Pamela longed for the Hollywood life, having heard of it from her Ostrer relatives, and she had long been convinced that it was the only place for James to live and work if he was ever going to make it as a world-class movie star. James himself now saw it as an increasingly attractive alternative to what he considered the hopelessly small-minded, parochial and bureaucratic activities of the Rank Organisation. While Hollywood had seen nothing exportable in James's run of costume villains, they found an altogether more attractive possibility in *The Seventh Veil*, and there was the immediate suggestion that he might like to travel out to Los Angeles for a meeting with the Hollywood mogul Spyros Skouras, naturally all expenses paid, to consider the possibility of a deal with Twentieth Century Fox. But James, having just escaped from his Gainsborough studio contract, was unwilling to shackle himself to another, even in Hollywood, and while he was debating with Pamela his chances of maintaining any kind of independent actor-producer career in his native land, and coincidentally contenting himself with yet more articles about the sheer awfulness of being an English film star, an offer came along which put any further thought of emigration well into the future.

Arguably the only truly great film that Mason ever made, and one already unwisely rejected by Stewart Granger, *Odd Man Out* was a screen version of F. L. Green's classic novel about an Irish rebel leader being hunted by the police after an armed robbery. The director Carol Reed, about to move on to *The Fallen Idol* and *The Third Man* but already recognized as one of the most important talents in the wartime film industry, had acquired the screen rights and commissioned a script from the author himself and the play-wright R. C. Sheriff, author of *Journey's End*. He came to the very early conclusion that he wanted Mason for the gunman on the run but would surround him with the local cream of Abbey Theatre players as the friends and enemies that he encounters on his short, poetic journey to the grave.

Shooting on *Odd Man Out* started early in 1946 with a month's location work in Belfast, where the Irish actor Dan O'Herlihy joined the unit to play one of the junior members of Mason's gun-running organization, a thinly-disguised variant of the IRA:

'I don't think any of us playing in that IRA cell – Cyril Cusack, Mason, Robert Beatty, me – were actually aware that we were making the best film of our lives but of course we were, because Carol Reed was a master psychologist who knew how to direct each of us best in quite different ways. We actually started that picture without the girl who shelters Mason and finally gives her life to die with him in the gunfire on the snow: there had been rumours of Ann Todd, but when that didn't work out Carol asked us if we knew of anyone. I'd just finished doing a college play in Belfast with Kathleen Ryan so I mentioned her and she played the part quite wonderfully.

'But it was really Carol's film: he knew exactly what he wanted each frame to look like and, apart from Robert Newton as the painter and Fay Compton as the woman who takes Mason into her home, he cast the whole picture locally in Belfast so it had this remarkable authenticity. And what made James so good, looking back on it, is that inside himself he was already on the run. He was very bitter about England, about the way they'd treated him as a conscientious objector, about the way the studio bosses seemed to want absolute power over their actors, and there was a very strong sense that he too was a rebel trying to get away from everything and everybody. He loved Ireland, remembered his days at the Gate with great affection, and I think he had a certain sympathy with the film, which really was one that you couldn't make today because, in effect, it painted an IRA killer in a very sympathetic light. It's possible to argue that James was almost too intellectual for his own good, but he had much more depth than most. Although he wasn't very emotional he could indicate emotion on screen superbly: there was an austere vulnerability about him which could be immensely powerful.'

Certain critics had doubts about *Odd Man Out*, and they were essentially to do with the fact that, as Roger Manvell noticed, 'the centre of gravity of the action, which is the pursuit of Mason, is not quite true to the centre of gravity of the film's theme, which is the revelation of human qualities against the final measure of good and evil'. But C.A. Lejeune for the *Observer* reckoned it quite simply 'a masterpiece', and there were even those who compared it to Greek tragedy in the way it remained almost true to the unity of time – the whole action occurs in the second half of a single day.

Many of the characters in *Odd Man Out* could have stepped straight from an O'Casey play: W.G. Fay as the gentle priest, Maureen Delany as the police informer, Newton himself as the over-the-top artist, F.J. McCormick as the old tramp, Dennis O'Dea as the policeman, all are in their way archetypal. What saved *Odd Man Out* from being just a postwar rerun of John Ford's *The Informer* was Reed's hard-edged English refusal to deal with any sentimental Celtic twilight. Mason's Johnny is not some great local anti-hero but a symbol of flight in an imperfect world, and the film was greater than the character because of that. As Paul Dehn wrote after a first screening, 'My boats are all burnt and my trumpets are ready for the sounding: this is the best picture I have ever seen.'

The intervening forty years have not been altogether kind to *Odd Man Out*. In the colder light of 1989, Robert Newton's alcoholic artist looks hopelessly stagey, and Reed's attempt to convey Mason's delirium through a collage of faces in beer bubbles looks uncharacteristically tricksy. And yet the parable still works in an almost biblical way: one scarcely notices that Mason plays more than half the story in total silence, reacting only to the words of others.

16

'Publicity-wise I made a poor start in New York: I really had nothing to say except that I quite liked the Rockefeller Center and didn't think it at all eccentric to have crossed the Atlantic with five cats and a sheepdog. It was a small sheepdog.'

THE FILMING OF *Odd Man Out* in Belfast somehow seemed to crystallize James's determination to become an exile himself. Despite the fact that offers were coming in from all studios, offers of one-picture deals which would not tie him down to another dreaded contract, none of them had the distinction of *Odd Man Out* and James had now begun to believe his own articles about the utter impossibility of the British film industry as a place for intelligent adults to make a living. Pamela was more than ever convinced that their future lay in Hollywood, and if there were ever a time to make such a move then it was surely while his Gainsborough pictures were forming queues all over New York.

So, enter David E. Rose, an American producer who had been running Paramount in England during the war and who now suggested that, with *Odd Man Out* poised to take America by storm, he and Mason should form their own production company, one which would allow James to choose his own subjects and shoot them with Hollywood money. With Spyros Skouras still on his doorstep offering everything from *Forever Amber* to *Anna and the King of Siam* (which went respectively to George Sanders and Rex Harrison after Mason turned them down), James nevertheless decided that he would rather go as an independent in partnership with Rose than as the employee of any studio, and even wrote a fatal letter to his prospective partner confirming their agreement.

There was from now onwards to be a sharp contrast between the public view of Mason's life and career and his own private estimate of it. While he was at the top of his English box-office fame, he had already begun to live in a kind of internal exile, convinced that the press and the studios were out to get him even at the moment when they were doing their best for him. Like Richard II, a role he ought to have played and never did, he put himself into a kind of banishment long before this was strictly necessary, as if going out to embrace the worst would somehow be better than waiting for it to come to him. Determined therefore to burn those few boats around English studios that he had as yet left unscorched, James wrote another magazine article announcing that he was leaving for Hollywood because it was 'demoralizing' to have J. Arthur Rank in charge of so much of British film-making, adding for good measure, 'Rank is the worst thing to have happened to British movie-making. He has so much money from his flour-milling business that he has been able to move in and absorb the whole industry. He is making the mistake of buying markets to expand his empire, and he doesn't seem to care how much it costs. He has no apparent talent for the cinema or showmanship, and Mr Rank has made the mistake of surrounding himself with a lot of quaint folk who know nothing about the creative side of film-making. The result is that creative artists are mishandled.'

All of which was very largely true, and could realistically only have been said in public by an actor on his way to catch the *Queen Elizabeth* at Southampton for American emigration, so powerfully did the Rank Organisation then control the lives of British film-makers. The problem was that precisely because he was now an emigrant, the Wardour Street press rallied behind those they would still have to live with and denounced Mason as an ungrateful malcontent, determined to bite the hands that had fed him an all-British stardom. One critic even suggested that his performance in *Odd Man Out* was simply not good enough to justify so rebellious an attitude towards his studio superiors, while others complained that there was something deeply unpatriotic about his departure for America at a moment when British films were again (and largely thanks to him) acquiring a kind of distinction. Intriguingly this was not a case ever made against such contemporary emigrants as Stewart Granger or Rex Harrison or Deborah Kerr, but then they had never dared go public with any attack on the ruling hierarchy of the home industry.

In departing for America towards the end of 1946, at precisely the moment when his British career was at a commercial and critical height which it would never recapture, there is no doubt that Mason did himself professional damage from which he took years, if not decades, to recover. But the problem was not simply caused by a crossing of the Atlantic: he was also going into a year-long wilderness of no film-making at all, and that, too, was largely trouble of his own creation. With the best of intentions but a hamfistedness that was breathtaking, James now set about the reconstruction of a career much like a dive-bomber setting about the restoration of his target by first razing everything else to rubble.

Even before he began packing for America, James had realized that the arrangement with David Rose was simply not going to work out. Rose had gone back to California ahead of him, but instead of setting up the kind of elegant and artistic projects that Mason had dreamed of, he was wiring back to England news of possible deals with a series of unsuitable studios for a number of unattractive projects. When he reappeared that autumn, it was with the news that he was proposing to sign Mason to a ten-picture deal at Paramount, one that would give James no production authority and no more control over his fate than he had enjoyed in England.

Firmly, James and Pamela indicated that their relationship with Rose was now at an end: there was, however, the matter of the letter of intent which James had signed a few months earlier, a letter confirming that he and Rose were to work together in Hollywood. In an amiably vague way, Mason now assumed that this could easily be cancelled; indeed he went so far as to agree a quite different deal with Alexander Korda who, at the eleventh hour, and with Mason's bags already halfway to Southampton (Pamela and James having decided that not even the falling-out with Rose would deprive them of the chance to inspect Hollywood possibilities), turned up on their doorstep with an offer vastly more attractive than anything Rose had managed to elicit in California.

Korda, who had not used Mason since the bit in *Fire Over England* a decade earlier, but had now belatedly awoken to his stardom, was offering a six-picture deal which would allow James to go to California, make the first films there, but retain a foothold in England where at least half the contract would be fulfilled. The offer could hardly have been better written by James himself: it opened the way to a transatlantic life, American experience, an escape from J. Arthur Rank and just about everything he had ever wished for, even in his most unreasonably querulous articles.

Armed therefore with the Korda offer, James gathered up Pamela, five cats, a staff of three, one sheepdog and a second-hand converted ambulance in which he proposed to drive his party from New York across America to Hollywood. At the Southampton quayside he announced to a few pressmen his intention of taking up the Korda offer. He had reckoned without David Rose, however: the Masons set foot on American soil five days later to be greeted by the news that Rose had slapped in a breach-of-contract suit demanding just over one million dollars or, failing that, an injunction to prevent James from selling his services to anyone else for at least the next two years. It was not the best of starts to a new American life.

17

'The author was sitting with his head in his hands and in the depths of depression: he had not expected the audience to laugh.'

THOSE VERSED IN the ways of Hollywood at once knew what David Rose was up to. According to their scenario, he never really expected a million-dollar settlement, nor least of all that James would seriously consider not working with any other film producer for two whole years at the very height of his new-found fame and bankability. This scenario assumes that Rose just wanted a bit of the action that was now flourishing around James; having got to him first, fully six months ahead of the field, he would now like to have been cut in for a small management percentage of whatever deal Korda was at last offering, and would have been happy to negotiate on that basis reasonably quickly. A legal suit for breach of contract was just the opening round in an already old-established Hollywood negotiating pattern. Surely everyone knew that?

Everyone, it would appear, but James: still cut off from his own family by what they saw as unpatriotic wartime pacifism and now by his equally unpatriotic decision to emigrate, Mason had also cut himself off from most English studio friends and contacts by his increasingly hostile attacks on J. Arthur Rank and his all-powerful organization. He was therefore chronically without advisers, in a new and foreign country, and surrounded as usual only by Pamela, whose instinct was, like his, to fight Rose every step of the way. It was a professionally disastrous instinct, and utterly typical of James at his most Yorkshire stubborn: seldom can a nose have been cut off quite so slowly to spite a face as it was in the next year of Mason's non-career.

The Masons docked in New York in December 1946, intending only to stay in the city for a matter of weeks before driving cross-country to California and James's new Hollywood prospect. In the event they stayed a year, which was about as long as it took for interest in him as a movie star to die quietly on both sides of the Atlantic. As usual, James did not make the best of starts with local journalists. Rumours that he was both 'difficult' and 'anti-studio' (this last being regarded as the greatest of all possible crimes at a time when long-term contracts were still obligatory) had preceded him from England, and he did not make things any better by immediately denying an interview to the gossip columnist Louella Parsons, who then spent the next two Sundays denouncing him on her coast-to-coast radio show as 'uncooperative' and 'swollen-headed'.

The David Rose struggle now took a new turn: instead of settling out of court, Mason had decided to counter-sue and was advised that his chances of this would be better in New York than Los Angeles. Accordingly James, Pamela and the entourage settled expensively in Greenwich, Connecticut, and, with no chance of any filming on that coast even if he had been free of the Rose lawsuit, Mason turned back somewhat reluctantly towards the theatre on Broadway where a good many of his prewar friends and acquaintances, from Rex Harrison to Robert Flemyng, now seemed to be making a successful living.

The play that James chose for his Broadway debut was *Bathsheba*, an unsatisfactory Jacques Deval biblical saga in which Pamela was to play the title role with James as King David. Deval had enjoyed one or two Broadway hits including *Tovarich*, but what made managements think they might get away with this copper-bottomed clinker was presumably the huge success that James was now enjoying around the cinemas of New York with *The Wicked Lady* and *Odd Man Out*. Movie critics were describing him as everything from 'repayment for Britain's war debts' to 'a glowering cinematic glamour boy' and 'England's cultured answer to Humphrey Bogart'.

Bathsheba was, however, in deep trouble from the moment it opened in Philadelphia and the audience began to laugh. A major row broke out between actors and author about whether the play was a biblical tragedy or a light comedy about ancient sexual mores. Audiences seemed equally uncertain, and although various directors and play-doctors were summoned and dispatched during the tryout, they were in such total chaos that on the closing matinée in Philadelphia one member of the audience actually joined the cast on stage to announce that in his view the show was a stinker.

A few days later, New York papers confirmed this amateur judgement of the piece and the production: Pamela struck one critic as 'an awful actress' and James struck another as 'monotonous and a trifle nasal', though this one did have the grace to describe him as a 'cinematinée idol'. *Newsweek* dwelt on the actor-author quarrel at some length: 'Deval wanted *Bathsheba* played for tragedy, while Mason saw it as an ironic comedy. The contest ended in a draw, with both contestants losing. *Bathsheba* as it opened on Broadway never achieves the drama inherent in King David's seducing the wife of Uriah, but nor does it derive any appreciable amount of sophisticated humour, and Mrs Mason, miscast in the title role, is unable to do much about it.' The *New York Daily News* summed up in its usual brisk fashion: 'James Mason makes mild debut in dullish Biblical sex comedy'. So now not only did James not have a Hollywood career, he didn't have a Broadway one either. He was only ever to make one more appearance there, just over thirty years later.

True to the Masons' usual stage tradition *Bathsheba* closed within the month, and although this would have been the moment for James to go speedily to Hollywood and cash in on his Gainsborough fame before it could get any more tarnished, he was by now tied to New York by the legal proceedings surrounding the David Rose suit and counter-suit, all of which promised to take a very long time to be resolved.

In the meantime, beached and out of work in Connecticut, James contented himself with casual journalism, mainly first impressions of America for English magazines and jovial little pieces on the difference between his *Wicked Lady* image and domestic reality (including one entitled 'Why I Beat My Wife'). For good measure, he also began attacking Hollywood producers as 'flesh peddlers' and announced that one of his new ambitions was to live in America without ever having to visit California, none of which deeply endeared him to the men he would have to work with for the next fifteen years of his life. 'Only Orson Welles', noted one columnist in grudging admiration, 'ever managed to make so many enemies quite so fast', while back in England the Rank Organisation severed all connections with a curt statement that 'Mr Mason doesn't speak to us any more; in fact, he barely speaks to anyone any more'.

Asked about his own screen performances, James said that he viewed almost all of them with 'a fascinated kind of horror'. This again was not the standard reply then being taught to movie stars by Hollywood publicity officers. He was, however, grudgingly prepared to admit that 'the sun shines longer and machinery works better' in America, and that he might therefore stay awhile.

With nothing else to do, and several weeks turning into months before the Rose suits could come to court, James did some New York radio shows including several for the comedian Fred Allen, after whose wife, Portland, the Masons were to name their first child. He also broadcast some dramas, including *Morning Glory*, and further attempted to make American ends meet by offering his memoirs to a local publisher. There seemed a lack of enthusiasm for these: James still fascinated the American press with his rare mixture of belligerence, acid wit, secrecy, ill-temper and intelligence, all unusual enough at a time when most movie stars did not even cough except through a press agent, but that fascination did not seem to extend to an entire book.

But this was the time when movie stars were closely associated with lovable animals (Elizabeth Taylor had just written a bestselling book about a tame chipmunk called Nibbles, though she was barely into her teens). The Masons found it easier to write and sell *The Cats in our Lives*, a twee little hardback about the various domestic pets they continued to crowd around them; not until the coming of Andrew Lloyd Webber forty years later, did anyone work harder to market cats to the media than James and Pamela.

But even the cosiness of that failed to rub off the hard edges that the press still found around James in this long and aimless time of transition between Pinewood and Hollywood; indeed, when first in America he achieved the rare distinction, remarkable even by James's standards of press hostility, of an unfavourable review in a restaurant menu. He had attacked the establishment's seating plans in one of his magazine columns, and the restaurant memorably retaliated by attacking his acting among its *plats du jour*.

By the autumn of 1947 it was clear even to James that he was getting precisely nowhere in New York: guest radio shots on Fred Allen could not begin to cover his living expenses, there was no money coming from England, and the fiasco of *Bathsheba* had put paid to any other Broadway hopes. With the Rose case still stalled in the New York courts, and the weather now moving into a winter of appalling snowdrifts, the Masons decided the time had come to continue their trek west in search of a place in the sun.

18

*'My Hollywood career eventually started with a straight
run of five failures, but though it may be hard to believe,
each choice I made was in fact the best available at the time.'*

ON THE RUN from the snows of the eastern seaboard, the Masons
first considered Bermuda but finally settled for Arizona, whence an
overpowering sense of boredom after about ten days sent them on
to California. Legally they were not supposed to be there at all, since
sight of Mason on Hollywood territory could trigger the serving of
yet another writ by David Rose. In characteristic and chaotic fashion,
James therefore took up his first Los Angeles residence on the strict
understanding that he was never to leave his rented accommodation
or be seen near a sidewalk or a supermarket, let alone a studio. He
was, true to his own still deeply confused sense of his career
prospects, in Hollywood but not really there.

This lunatic cloak-and-dagger life luckily didn't last for more than
a few weeks, at which point a New York judge at last gave it as his
opinion that no binding contract existed between Rose and Mason,
and that therefore Mason was now free to seek work with any studio
he liked in Hollywood. All that had been lost by James was one year
of his professional life and several thousand dollars in legal fees.

But even now he was determined to stand by many of the principles with which he had left England to make a new life for himself:
he would not sign any kind of a studio contract, nor take on any
assignment with which he was not in total artistic sympathy and

preferably allowed some sort of control. Nowadays that is the credo of most working actors, even in California. In 1948, it was regarded as the policy of a dangerously anti-studio foreign rebel, and as a result Mason was almost immediately thrown in with a ragged group of other European exiles in Hollywood, few of whom had anything more to unite them than a sense of alienation from the prevailing American studio ethic.

The problem for James was that, always a loner, he had nothing in common with his fellow English in California, and not much in common with the native Americans either. His wartime pacifism and a general disenchantment with the Britain he had left behind scarcely equipped him to join such surviving members of the Hollywood Raj as Ronald Colman, David Niven and Deborah Kerr, gathered around the cricket club that had once been run by Sir C. Aubrey Smith. On the other hand, a deep and fastidious horror of the commercialism of the American dream meant that he could hardly go native like Errol Flynn, Peter Lawford or Elizabeth Taylor. He was, as usual, the odd man out of time and place, and his instinctive, immediate loathing for Los Angeles was only matched by the passion with which Pamela fell in love with it.

And there was another problem: whereas at Gainsborough James had been able to corner the market in gentlemanly brooding villains, out in California earlier settlers from England such as Herbert Marshall, Claude Rains and even George Sanders had been doing some very similar work since the late 1930s. A decade later they were mostly established on the kind of studio contracts that would give them first pick of any roles which came up in Mason's specific area of screen expertise, snobbery with violence.

It took James remarkably little time to fall in with other intellectual European misfits in California, such as Max Ophuls (for whom he made two of his first three Hollywood films) and Wolfgang Reinhardt, both of whom still seemed to believe that freelance art films were possible under the studio sun. Their first plan was to make an Arthur Laurents script called *Caught*, in which Mason was scheduled at first to play an evil tycoon loosely based on Howard Hughes. Determined to shatter his wartime image of the sinister heavy, James insisted on playing the lesser role of a poor young doctor who falls in love with the tycoon's wife, ceding to Robert Ryan the more flamboyant part. Max Ophuls collapsed with an attack of shingles during the shooting, and the result was a fair old disaster, as Mason later told a radio interviewer: 'People always ask me why I chose to start my Hollywood career with *Caught*, thinking that I was in a position to choose whatever film I wanted. I used to make up some important-sounding reason, like having to work with Ophuls or being fascinated by the script. The truth of the matter was that I was desperately broke, needed a job, and this was the nearest thing to an acceptable project that was offered to me ... at least it would be a decent little film, nothing cheap or vulgar. The problem was that Ophuls insisted on having a dialogue director as well as himself, and then the censor insisted on script changes, and the whole thing just ended up as a terrible mess.'

By now John Monaghan, an American army captain James and Pamela had first met during the last of their wartime troop tours, had joined their Hollywood household, which was also soon to be enlarged by the arrival of their first child, Portland, in November 1948, and then by Pamela's first husband, Roy Kellino, who came out to live with them again and to start a new career in American television. Friends have always talked about James getting more and more withdrawn as his years went by in Hollywood; the truth may just have been that the house simply got noisier, reflecting Pamela's intense sociability rather than his own innate desire for escape into himself.

Yet the Masons' passion for opening up their home to resident guests caused considerable American press speculation, most of which centred initially on the rather mysterious presence of Monaghan: 'After his discharge from the army at the end of the war,' wrote one Hollywood reporter, 'he seems to have become the Masons' inseparable companion. A small part was found for him in *The Upturned Glass* and Pamela has dedicated her latest novel *Ignoramus, Ignoramus*, the last of the four that she published in the 1940s to him. Monaghan is a burly, black-haired type, and strangers have taken him for a bodyguard. Actually, whether in film studios or sharing hotel suites with the Masons, Monaghan seems to be more of a friendly handyman than anything else. He attends them both with a doggish sort of devotion, runs errands and does odd jobs impartially for them both, and recently announced that he might start work on a biography of Mason [he did in fact publish an extended magazine profile at the end of the 1940s]. At home he

College days: James (standing second from right) with his Cambridge crew at Peterhouse in the summer of 1929

In the Old Vic season at Sadler's Wells, 1934: James seated background left with Elsa Lanchester, Marius Goring and the cast of Tyrone Guthrie's revival of *The Tempest*

With Elsa Lanchester and the cast of *The Cherry Orchard*, Old Vic 1933/34

With Charles Laughton and Flora Robson in *Henry VIII* (James standing centre right), 1934

Gainsborough to Rank to Hollywood: the early screen idol

With Margaret Lockwood as *The Wicked Lady* (1945): 'the hoary, the tedious and the disagreeable are married with an infelicity rare even in costume pictures' (*Sunday Times*)

With Ann Todd in *The Seventh Veil* (1945): 'James Mason registers another hit as a fascinating brute' (*Daily Express*)

James Mason and Ann Todd suggest in *The Seventh Veil* 'a passion that is strong and selfless' (*The Times*)

With Pamela Kellino Mason in *The Upturned Glass* (1947)

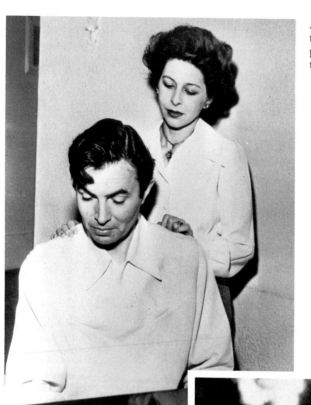

At home and at work with Pamela: the film was the one they wrote, produced, acted and financed themselves, *I Met a Murderer*

Alone and with Robert Newton in *Odd Man Out* (1947), the film that James and many others always reckoned his best: it was directed by Carol Reed

And so to Hollywood: James and Pamela with their daughter Portland

generally sits by them in happy silence, consuming double Scotches and watching for the slightest chance to serve them or their guests. When he speaks of himself and the Masons he always says 'us' or 'we', and when someone recently referred to Pamela's first husband Roy Kellino in Monaghan's presence, he replied with complete aplomb, "Yeah, we still see him sometimes.".'

But James had more to worry about than whether local Californian scribes found his living arrangements unconventional: his unwavering decision to go it alone, far from giving him the protection of any studio salary, meant that he would have to survive from film to film, and even though he could be sure of getting five or even ten times the money he had been getting per picture in England – which had never even in the Gainsborough days risen above £10,000 a script – this would only hold good so long as his last picture was a success. In that context, *Caught* had not been the most reassuring of starts.

It was followed by *Madame Bovary*, which once again Mason embarked on by declining the role offered to him and selecting instead a minor one as the author himself. 'I was very much impressed by the Robert Ardrey script, especially as *Bovary* had always seemed to me impossible to translate into film terms. I didn't think I would do very well with Bolenger, which eventually went to Louis Jourdan, but I asked if I could play Flaubert in the introduction and at the end. So off we went, and I was still such a hero in those days, as *Caught* had not yet been released and my English pictures were still all over California, that the director Vincente Minnelli just left me alone. The trouble is that I was still a very lazy actor, and I just thought things would happen automatically if I gave a typically lazy performance; then I saw the film and realized that my first instinct had been right and that *Bovary* was quite impossible on the screen. It never has worked as a film and it never will, but on that occasion I certainly didn't help it.'

By now, James had decided that American studios were not all they were cracked up to be, and he'd already begun to write irritable articles for English newspapers complaining of a lack of good directors and of the unhealthy power enjoyed by the producers, precisely the same accusations that he'd been levelling against the Rank Organisation five years earlier. A rare and early Hollywood friend of James's, the director Preston Sturges, explained that for survival in Beverly Hills two quite different talents were required: 'First you have to have talent as an artist; secondly you have to have talent as a strategist and diplomat.' James was undoubtedly qualified on the first count, but he remained chronically deficient in that second talent. It was a deficiency which could only be overcome by the kind of box-office success that he was now patently unable to deliver.

19

'I remember two things about Pandora: *the brilliance of Jack Cardiff's cinematography and the resultant embellishment of Ava Gardner's great natural beauty.'*

MASON'S EARLY HOLLYWOOD career continued in a welter of lawsuits: the David Rose affair was no sooner settled than it was announced that James and Pamela would be suing, for a million dollars, a gossip writer who had speculated that their marriage might be in trouble. Even Portland's christening developed into a punch-up with the press when James took understandable objection to a cameraman trying to take flash pictures next to the font. In many ways a gentle, shy and retiring man, he was managing the local papers with all the delicacy of a prizefighter; he even contrived to make it into the society columns a few months later for hitting William Saroyan in a downtown cinema when Saroyan refused to stop talking during a screening of John Huston's *The Red Badge of Courage.*

Sadly, however, Mason's private life was proving far more dramatic than anything he was able to achieve on screen. Though he had managed to get $20,000 a day for his one week's work on *Madame Bovary,* more than that was still needed to pay off the legal costs on the Rose affair and set up a Hollywood home for himself and Pamela, their new daughter, Monaghan and assorted retainers and guests, not to mention the traditional but still growing menagerie of half a dozen cats and a newly arrived poodle.

James went straight on into another Max Ophuls disaster, even allowing himself this time to revert to screen type and play the suave blackmailer falling in love with Joan Bennett, his victim. English reviews were vitriolic ('Mason has no one to blame but himself: he was the one who chose to go and live in Hollywood, and he was the one who chose to make a film as bad as *The Reckless Moment*), and it was left to C. A. Lejeune in the *Observer* to wonder what on earth was happening to Mason in his new Californian existence: 'Here is an actor who withdrew from this country as soon as it became apparent that British fans were clamorous to see him, and he must indeed be one of the shyest men in pictures. Since his arrival in America, he appears to have developed a Harry Lime complex: not only does he eschew the close-up, dodging recognition in the shadows, generally muffled in a long overcoat, but he seems reluctant to turn up on the screen at all. The total duration of his public appearances in the three films he has made in Hollywood must be something like thirty minutes. In the first, *Caught,* he sidled onto the screen in a retiring way when the story was already half over. In the second, *Madame Bovary,* he did no more than address a few introductory and closing remarks to the audience. In the third, *The Reckless Moment*, he arrives late and thereafter only intermittently, usually in a bad light and a considerable hurry.'

Others were still tougher. 'Mason was once our brightest star,' wrote a *Daily Express* critic, 'but in the Hollywood firmament he glimmers only very wanly. Indeed in his latest film he doesn't crop up until half an hour has elapsed, and need not really have appeared at all. That for his own sake might have been best.'

To the acrid smell of burning bridges, Mason lurched on through two more B-thriller disasters. *East Side, West Side* had him caught between Ava Gardner and Barbara Stanwyck, but is only famous now for being the film on which a small-part player called Nancy Davis got introduced by her director to an actor from a neighbouring set by the name of Ronald Reagan. Like James's next, *One Way Street* with Dan Duryea, it turned up briefly in London to yet more shouts of gleeful derision from those Wardour Street critics who still seemed to believe that a slow professional death in minor Hollywood thrillers was a suitable fate for the man who had dared to criticize J. Arthur Rank and the whole establishment of British movie-making.

But James was still not averse to biting the few hands still willing to feed him. After a year of unemployment on screen followed by five commercial disasters back to back, he was still prepared to announce that 'the English colony in Hollywood cut pathetic figures with their clothes, accent and cricket. I have no wish to be one of them'. Why, then, was he so intent on staying? 'Well, the climate for one thing, and my wife and little daughter seem to love the house. I'm not even sure that if I'd stayed in Britain I'd have done much better work: you don't get an *Odd Man Out* or a Carol Reed coming along every day of the week.'

Ironically, the first postwar film that James made with American money and any real chance of success was to be largely shot in England. Towards the end of 1950, MGM approached him with the offer of a major picture, apparently unperturbed by the box-office damage he had recently been doing in minor ones; this was to be *Pandora and the Flying Dutchman*, a screen treatment by Albert Lewin (as producer/director/writer) of the legend about the sailor doomed for eternity to roam the seas, but allowed to live the life of a human for six months every seven years, in the hope that the true love of a girl willing to die for him might expiate his sins.

Whether Lewin was prescient enough to see in James's melancholic and restless soul an ability to make sense of a peripatetic quest quite as daft as that of the Flying Dutchman, or whether he was just in need of a star willing to do a lot of European location shooting at a time when most were still reluctant to leave the Californian sun, is not really of any great importance: James landed the role, started shooting on Costa Brava coastline and finished up in a Shepperton studio gazing soulfully into the eyes of Ava Gardner.

Even there, however, he was seldom free from trouble. No sooner had he set foot on British soil than Sir Alexander Korda reappeared from his past, offering this time not a starring role but an arguable claim for fifty thousand dollars which Korda said he had advanced to Mason for two films that were never made. Beyond that, and a ritual fracas with the British press when it was announced that he and Pamela were to seek American citizenship, the *Pandora* filming was uneventful, though even James must have been aware that in 1950 his was a less than spectacular homecoming. 'It was a terrible waste of petrol,' wrote a *News Chronicle* critic, 'to have a car kill James Mason at the end of his last film *One Way Street*. Another couple of films like that and the job could have been done without a car.' Mason swiftly replied with a checklist of what really mattered to him in films:

'1: to enjoy the work; 2: to make a film I like; 3: to be paid for it; 4: to be liked by those who see it; 5: to be liked by critics. With all my American films I have scored 1 and 3. With *The Reckless Moment* I also scored 2, and on *Caught* I was able to add 4. Number 5 has eluded me as consistently in America as it did in England.'

And yet there was one great difference between James's public standing in 1946 in Britain and that to which he returned in 1950. In 1946 he was heading all box-office charts for the third year in succession: in 1950 those charts were led by Richard Todd, John Mills and Michael Wilding, and Mason featured nowhere on any of them. 'I am therefore now hoping,' wrote James, 'that I may have liquidated my news value, in which case both I and the British reading public may relax with the comfortable assurance that neither they nor I will ever have to open our newspapers again in fear of encountering some idiotic reference to the Mason cats.'

That, however, was not to be. Something about Mason's arrogance, or his intelligence, or maybe just his continuing desire for independence, seemed to irritate journalists far outside the review columns. On the day that he announced his intention to seek American citizenship, the *People* ran across the top of their editorials an unsigned leader which concluded, 'I do protest loudly at the intolerable patronage of a Mr James Mason, who obviously thinks America is a nicer place to live than England and openly declares that it is a better place for making pictures. Not that I grudge America the addition of this tiny shooting star to its otherwise nobly spangled banner. Unlike coal and nylon stockings, he is an export we can very well do without at home.'

Mason now badly needed the success that *Pandora* might possibly give him; true to his usual critical luck, the raves on it came in just thirty years after its first release.

20

'Although The Desert Fox *and* Five Fingers *did well, it looked as if the honeymoon was over for serious films aimed at a discriminating audience.'*

WHEN *Pandora* first opened on both sides of the Atlantic early in 1951, reviews were at best lukewarm; the general feeling was that it looked wonderful, that Marius Goring and Nigel Patrick were strong in support, but that, as the London *Times* critic noted, 'Mr Mason gets very little help from Miss Gardner, whose acting consists of a series of star poses, or indeed from a script of quite incredible pretentiousness which every now and again demands that Mr Mason recite what Miss Gardner persists in calling "a pome" ... the film is conspicuous on its confident assumption of scholarship, and in its utter poverty of taste and imagination.'

For the *Observer*, C. A. Lejeune went further: 'The sad thing about *Pandora* is that, in spite of its merits, the final grace of taste and dignity is missing. In ten years' time, in five years, even in one year, I dare swear that the film will have been junked from every connoisseur's collection. I am sorry to think that our country will be blamed for its inadequacy: in a technical sense the thing is undoubtedly British, but in a deeper sense it is no more British or European than the samba, the jukebox or the rye highball.'

In the event, the verdict of film history went in exactly the opposite direction to that forecast by Lejeune: after a disappointing few years at the box office, during which time Mason never saw any money at all from the profit percentage he had been promised for the simple reason that there was no profit, *Pandora* began to emerge from a watery grave and turn up at film-society screenings. By 1985 it was being hailed at the ICA by Alexander Walker as 'a masterpiece of unconscious kitsch, a film as monstrously, adorably, munificently bad as any that I've seen'. It became, in short, a collector's piece.

It also led Mason into the one golden period of his fifteen Hollywood years: over the next four years he was to make his two Rommel movies as well as *Five Fingers*, *Julius Caesar* and *A Star is Born*, among half a dozen lesser pictures, thereby establishing the run of success which he had hoped for since the end of the war.

The first Rommel picture, *Desert Fox*, actually arose from the *Pandora* shooting. On a nearby Shepperton set was the Hollywood producer Nunnally Johnson, who had already beaten James to buy the film rights to the new Desmond Young biography of the German general, in which Mason had quickly seen a marvellous role for himself. Twentieth Century Fox agreed that he would be the right actor for the part, but before work on that could begin there was another disaster to be made.

This was *The Lady Possessed*, a curious little adventure which James and Pamela decided to keep in the family by making it themselves under the banner of 'Portland Pictures'. It was based on a novel of Pamela's about a concert pianist (to be played by James) and his suicidal lover. They completed the shooting on 'poverty row' at Republic, back in California, castastrophically using their own money, and opened it to reviews of breathtaking awfulness on both sides of the Atlantic. 'Dreary and meaningless twaddle,' thought the *New York Times*, adding 'this bleak little drama of neuroses is, we are candidly told, based on a novel by Pamela Kellino. Since she and Mr Mason also appear in the film and take credit for writing the script, the much celebrated couple have only themselves to blame.' *Variety* was equally appalled: 'A sordid and unpleasant little story during which Mason sings three tunes in a hoarse croon. His vocalizing is as unpleasant as the rest of the film.'

James and Pamela were by now accustomed to getting savage albeit possibly deserved reviews for anything they did together, and though there was henceforth to be a rapidly dwindling number of these joint projects, it says something of his continuing love for her that for more than a decade James allowed himself to be caught up time and again in a Kellino disaster of one kind or another. This one was especially painful because they had spent the best part of six months after *Pandora* first raising the money to make the film, then persuading June Havoc to play it, and finally hiring Roy Kellino when Havoc's then husband, who should have been the director, failed to acquire the right work permits.

Meanwhile, *Rommel – Desert Fox* was happily shaping up as Mason's first real Hollywood success in the three years since he had arrived there, though this too ran into some trouble on its first release from those who thought the screenplay too favourable to the Nazi leader. The critic and biographer, Leonard Mosley noted that he 'wished to throw hand grenades at the screen' for the way in which the film dismissed Montgomery's achievements in the western desert, and from Glasgow through Vienna to New York there were street protests from Jewish ex-servicemen about what they saw as the 'glorification' of Rommel.

Still, there was general agreement that the film brought Mason back from the wilderness into the glow of a box-office hit. Twentieth Century Fox overcame their shock-horror at his earlier refusal to make either *Young Bess* or *The Forsyte Saga* sufficiently to offer him a short-term studio contract. James abandoned his usual principles to accept it on the grounds that he had a wife and daughter to support, the fiasco of *The Lady Possessed* still to pay for, and no other work in the offing. By now California gossips had overcome their curiosity about Monaghan as a live-in guest of the Masons, and were focusing on the return to the household of Roy Kellino. 'It is safe to say that the home life of the Masons is unusual even for Hollywood,' wrote a local gossip-columnist Lon Jones, 'and their design for living resembles the plot of a sophisticated comedy, the sophistication being provided by Mrs Mason's ex-husband who lives in a guest house on the estate but seems to be very much a part of their daily lives as well as a partner in their Portland film company ... everything about the Mason ménage seems to be unusual, even little Portland who has now supplanted the cats in her father's affection. Though only two, she keeps theatrical hours, staying up until midnight so that she can see her father on his return from the studios and then sleeping all morning. Such hours might horrify most parents, but Porty seems to thrive on them and is far brighter and more precocious than others of her age.'

By now, and partly as an act of homage, James had moved his family and retainers into the former home of his great silent-screen hero Buster Keáton, and even set about the restoration of some old films of his that had been found in the attic. Pamela frequently referred in public to the house as 'a mausoleum', but it was she rather than James who had immediately taken to the local life, as her half-sister Diana de Rosso explains:

'Whether because she was Jewish, or just because she was a very strong and dynamic and dominant woman rather ahead of her time in those pre-feminist days, Pamela had always felt desperately out of place in her native England before the war, even among her own family who had been so terribly unhelpful to her about the release of *I Met a Murderer*. Somehow they never wanted to see her succeed, and she never felt accepted or encouraged to make her own name, whereas in California she suddenly found herself surrounded by people rather like her, people determined to make their names. She ended up with her own chat show out there and then dealing in property, and somehow it was a life ideally suited to her, whereas James began quite quickly to be horrified by the American dream of success. She was the one who liked pulling the strings, and James was hopelessly puppet-like: he allowed himself to be manipulated by her because I think he knew that he'd never make it by himself. He lacked the driving ambition which she possessed, and in America that became more and more evident, especially as Pamela was then in her element and James seemed more and more out of it all, which is why he withdrew into himself. You'd suddenly realize in the middle of one of their parties that he'd gone off to his study to be alone. Ever since Pam had first met American soldiers on that last wartime tour she'd found a warmth that she could never find at home, and she seemed to understand America right away, whereas James always remained characteristically doubtful and uncertain. I don't think he was ever really happy there; one or two films satisfied him, but that was the most he'd ever allow. On the other hand there didn't seem anything to come home for, and he now had not only his wife and daughter but also Roy who was still, in a way, his great friend out there, and one of the few he could really talk to.'

Another great friend of these early Californian years was the actor George Sanders, with whom Mason shared not only on-screen similarity among charming movie villains but also an off-screen, melancholic European intelligence which led them both to form a dim view of Hollywood social life. They even for a while half-seriously considered giving up acting and setting up in the building trade, where Mason would at last be able to use his architectural First from Cambridge and Sanders thought he would be able to charm wealthy local widows into commissioning vast mansions from the two of them.

In this last phase of the Hollywood Raj, the survivors were beginning to stick together and check each other over for signs of professional decay. 'Much in demand, old man?' Sanders would occasionally demand of Mason, knowing they had almost certainly been up for the same roles. 'In those days,' wrote James later, 'the main body of us Hollywoodites did not rapidly spiral upwards or downwards, we just sort of stood still until suddenly overcome by inertia.'

For now, however, there was a burst of activity generated by *Rommel*, from which Fox put him straight into an above-average spy drama called *Five Fingers*, based on the real-life story of an Albanian valet who worked as a double agent at the British embassy in Ankara during the war. Here James was able to give one of his most polished and expertly suave performances, much helped by a Joe Mankiewicz production which ought to have been the envy of Hitchcock himself.

21

'Juxtaposed with John Gielgud I must say I felt depressingly feeble, especially in the vocal department.'

THE DOUBLE SUCCESS OF *Rommel* and *Five Fingers* led James on to precisely nothing else: with his usual unlucky timing, he had made the last two hugely successful black-and-white movies in an industry that was now fleeing headlong into colour. In a Hollywood still desperately afraid of its own immediate past, he must have felt like the last silent star still trying to work through the advent of the talkies.

As at an earlier time in his life when there was no film work around, just before the war in England, Mason turned again towards television and began, with Pamela, to set up a company, which would make a series of half-hour dramas that could also be stitched together in threes and sold to cinemas as ninety-minute omnibus movies. While this was still on the drawing board, however, he got an offer from MGM to go into a remake of *The Prisoner of Zenda* as the evil Rupert of Hentzau, a role Raymond Massey had played definitively in the 1937 Ronald Colman classic. MGM themselves seemed to be aware that the first talking version of the story could hardly be improved on, and set up Moviolas on the set so that it could be studied shot by shot and faithfully recreated by the new cast. The actress Jane Greer recalls:

'I was playing the old Mary Astor role and the director told me I had to copy her every move and intonation, which I guess is why the film was so dreadful. James was the only one who refused to work like that, and so in his scenes I was all right because we actually rehearsed them properly and didn't just try for an accurate replica. He was a lovely, very quiet and sweet man who somehow managed to get his own way by just going very gently down his own path and not really taking notice of anyone in his way. I do remember he was always talking about Portland who was then about three, and about how he and Pamela had decided the only way to stop her smoking cigarettes in later life was to let her have one very young and see how it made her cough. So I asked how that had worked out and James said, "Well, she's now up to two packs a day".'

For Stewart Granger in the old Colman double role, *Zenda* was also something of a mistake, though it did at least reunite him briefly with his old wartime co-star from Gainsborough: 'In a way,' says the Hollywood columnist Roderick Mann, 'they were both rather alike, English loners in Hollywood desperate to do better work than the studios were then allowing them, but somehow unable to fit in totally with the local community or to form their own in the way that their predecessors in the earlier *Zenda* always had. They didn't even seem to get terribly close to each other, and whenever you saw them on the screen or at parties they always vaguely looked as though they wished they had gone somewhere else. I think that's perhaps why the Americans never quite warmed to them in the way they had to previous generations of the English abroad.'

From *Zenda*, with his career still on hold, James went into a curious project known as 'the New Screen Idea: the Duodrama'. The thinking behind it appears to have been that a public which would no longer sit through two bad movies in a double feature might still put up with them if they were telescoped into no more than ninety minutes altogether. Mason duly appeared in a Joseph Conrad short story before giving way to Robert Preston in a western. Following that there was a brief flurry of press excitement when it was widely rumoured that Greta Garbo had expressed yet another intention of returning to the screen, only this time 'in something with Mason'. Quite what that might be never transpired, and James returned instead to his television project, working on four short scripts of which three were eventually to gain a limited cinema release as *Charade*, a title not to be confused with the Stanley Donen classic of a decade or so later.

Mason's *Charade* was nothing if not a family affair: he and Pamela wrote all the scripts, John Monaghan played a small role, Roy Kellino directed and the result was, as James himself noted, 'a curiosity which I had hoped would be lost without trace'. When they were originally shown on American television the individual dramas had done little for ratings either, but they did give James a sort of taste for the small screen. In later years in New York he was to work for Sidney Lumet on vastly more distinguished television dramatizations of Robert Shaw's *The Hiding Place* and a new version of the Harper's Ferry story which he had originally done as a West End play but was known this time as *John Brown's Raid*.

Mason seemed doomed for a while to work only on very short projects: *Charade* even had to leave out one of the half-hour television dramas (another family affair, this one starring a four-year-old Portland who was reckoned by one English critic to have 'a dreadful American accent') which was released to cinemas independently. From that James went straight on to yet another omnibus, *The Story of Three Loves,* in one part of which he played a jealous impresario opposite the ballerina Moira Shearer in an odd rehash of *Red Shoes*.

Away from the studios, James was largely occupied in sending telegrams of apology to almost every other actor in Beverly Hills, most of whom he and Pamela had managed to affront in the course of a hilarious interview during which they were asked for their honest opinion of the local social scene. 'I guess we're not chi-chi enough to make that smart, ultra-British set, the type that play games,' said Pamela. 'They include Ronald Colman, Brian Aherne, Richard Greene and the Charles Boyers. That set's head mogul is Doug Fairbanks junior ...' 'The only guy in Hollywood with tails,' interposed James. 'Then there are the breeders,' said Pamela, 'and to get into that set your main hobby has to be raising children. Among them are the Bob Mitchums and the Bing Crosbys. You'll probably never get to meet Zsa Zsa Gabor unless you're in the executive-and-money set with the Darryl Zanucks and the Sam Goldwyns. Rita Hayworth leads the bachelorette set, but those gals really hate women and when they're not out with their current romance they're home with the mirror. People like Joan Crawford and Shelley Winters and Marilyn Monroe are culture vultures who spend their time reading the covers of books, and if you collect birds' skeletons or take crème de menthe in your morning coffee then you'll probably be allowed into the Bohemian set, which is led by Charles Laughton and Igor Stravinsky.'

Even by the Masons' usual press standards this one caused real trouble among the neighbours, to such an extent that they had to publish a full apology and sack their press agent. 'There is,' as Pamela wonderfully noted, 'really no point in paying somebody when we can get such bad publicity all by ourselves.'

Professionally, Mason now made a rapid return to Rommel: only two years after *Desert Fox* it had been decided to make *The Desert Rats*, which would attempt to right the balance by retelling the same North African campaign story but from a more British point of view. The role of Rommel was greatly reduced, while Richard Burton and Robert Newton starred as two English soldiers serving with the Australian army, but Mason was determined to retain his hold on the Desert Fox even if only for a couple of brief scenes. 'I felt that if I failed to play Rommel again they might hire a real German actor, and then my original performance would have been held up to question.'

It was only then, and not before time, that one of his rare Hollywood classics came along, largely thanks to the director Joe Mankiewicz for whom he had made *Five Fingers*:

'I always said that James was one of the great genuine eccentrics, because he never knew quite how eccentric he was. He always wished to be someplace else, but could never quite decide where that someplace was, or why he wanted to be there. He felt desperately unfulfilled by everything, and there was an inner man in him as in all of us, only in him it was never struggling to get out, just to stay inside. When we were starting on *Julius Caesar* for MGM in 1953 I knew that he was the Brutus I wanted. Not just because he'd once played it on the stage in Ireland, but because he was very complex and broody and unhappy, and that was precisely the Brutus I needed, a man who looked as though he belonged on a lonely battlefield. I insisted in my contract that we make it in black and white, even though colour was then all the rage, because I knew that if we shot in colour the assassination scene would be nothing but a great bloody mess on the screen, and the audience would be looking at the blood instead of at the face of Brutus and that was the heart of the film.

There was always a romantic sadness about James which was just perfect.'

Mason was considerably less confident about himself, though his uneasiness about being paired with Sir John Gielgud as Cassius was totally unfounded, as Gielgud says: 'James had much more to teach me on that film than I had to teach him. I used to observe his technique in the close-ups, and saw how brilliantly he expressed the character's thoughts without making faces or grimacing ... I thought his Brutus was underrated by most critics, since it is certainly the most difficult part in the play. He was extremely kind and generous to me; we were the only Englishmen in the cast, but he had not been to England for a long time and I was afraid they would all think I was this star actor from London who had come over to teach them Shakespeare, so I kept my mouth shut and we all got on very well together.' When shooting started Mason seemed especially nervous, as its producer John Houseman recalls:

'Actually I owe Mason a whole chunk of my later career, as he was to have played the Professor in the *Paper Chase* series – only he got delayed on a film so they gave the role to me. But at the time of *Caesar* he was feeling very rusty, hadn't done any Shakespeare for years, and it took him a day or two to get back into his stride. There's no doubt that Gielgud could handle the verse better, but James was one of those very rare screen actors like Gary Cooper and Alan Ladd, who always looked so much better in the daily rushes than they had on the studio floor. Brutus requires an absolute credibility as well as a sense of moral superiority, and James managed to deliver all of that.'

Not, however, without a struggle: at the first studio read-through, Houseman remembers, 'Gielgud, justly celebrated as the finest reader of verse on the English-speaking stage, just sailed through the part of Cassius with terrifying bravura; Mason, both depressed and embarrassed by the brilliance of his compatriot, chose to read the entire role of Brutus with a pipe clenched firmly in between his front teeth.'

Marlon Brando as Mark Antony had been a third choice after both Richard Burton and Paul Scofield proved unavailable. Despite Brando (some would say because of him; I am not one of them), the film worked out well enough, many critics even in Britain reckoning it more successful than the previous Shakespearean movies of

Olivier. MGM were taking no chances at the box office: 'A Story Greater Even Than *Ivanhoe*,' read the posters, and for Gielgud on his first Hollywood assignment the whole project was rich in local eccentricities. 'All right, kids,' he once heard an assistant director exhorting a crowd of recalcitrant extras before the shooting of the Forum scene, 'it's hot, it's Rome and here comes Julius.' On another occasion, Gielgud recalled, 'I was waiting to go onto the Rome street set with a whole menagerie of sheep, dogs and pigeons which had been brought in to make the city look more lively ... one of the pigeons left its perch and began walking around the floor of the studio, whereupon a hefty cowboy who had evidently been hired to look after all the animals dashed up and yelled at the bird, "Get back! Get back to your place! Don't you want to work tomorrow?" '

22

'For me the whole thing was a great treat, and I had this enormous admiration, a sort of love, for Judy Garland.'

UNLIKE JOHN GIELGUD, who could and did return after *Julius Caesar* to the English classical havens of the Old Vic and Stratford, James was still stuck in California and with whatever rubbish the studios chose to offer him next. Any illusions that Brutus might lift his career onto a more distinguished cinematic or artistic level must have been rapidly dashed by the *Botany Bay* with which James immediately followed *Caesar*. 'At its worst', as he later wrote, 'my Hollywood life was a matter of facile assembly work like *Botany Bay* or *The Prisoner of Zenda*: everything was very well-organized, and there was no audible griping.' Except, of course, from the critics, who still found it hard to come to terms with the rapid ups and downs of Mason's American career. *Botany Bay* was definitely a down. The story of a convict ship bound for eighteenth-century Australia, it starred Alan Ladd as an unjustly convicted highwayman and James as the ship's cruel captain, in what could only be considered a rehearsal for the Bligh he never got to play in any of the *Mutiny on the Bounty* remakes.

Then, after voicing a cartoon animation of Edgar Allan Poe's *The Tell-Tale Heart* and thereby sowing the seeds of what was in later life to prove a lucrative subsidiary career in commentaries, narrations and voice-overs with some of the most mellow and immediately identifiable tones in the business, there came a definite up: the chance to return to England and to work against with Sir Carol Reed, the director who had given him his greatest critical success to date in *Odd Man Out*.

This time Reed was planning to do for Berlin in *The Man Between* much what he had done for Vienna in *The Third Man*: to suggest that on the East–West political borderlines of central Europe there might exist a kind of moral no-man's-land, where frontiers were emotional states of mind as well as postwar realities. As Ivo Kern, a former lawyer now working in the East Berlin black market and enticing wanted men over the border, Mason was clearly being asked to play a variant of Harry Lime. Even his first appearance in the film is set up in much the same way as that of Orson Welles in the earlier classic.

But the problem was not just that a director is seldom at his best when revisiting scenes of past triumphs; it was also that on *The Third Man* they had had the benefit of Graham Greene's acid storytelling, where on *The Man Between* all they had was a faint carbon copy by an amiable Hollywood hack called Harry Kurnitz. So, despite a strong cast, including Claire Bloom and Hildegarde Neff, the film never lived up to the promise of its predecessor; it was minutely and wonderfully observed, but the banal storyline simply could not sustain Reed's wealth of visual detail, and Mason's German accent was not the only thing that was unconvincing. Still, he noted that the film worked well enough in an afterlife on late-night television, 'where no one demands of a thriller that the narrative thread be very taut'.

Though there were still snide references in the London press to his announced decision to take out American nationality, it was noticeable on Mason's return to London that a certain rapprochement was beginning. James and Pamela travelled to Yorkshire to show Portland to her grandparents, and for the first time since his decisions to live with Pamela and refuse to fight the war, therefore for the first time in fourteen years, he was again on speaking terms with the rest of the Mason family.

But his work was still in Hollywood, and it was there that he now returned for three major pictures in quick succession, of which only the first was really a mistake. *Prince Valiant* was the first CinemaScope swashbuckler, and it made a star of Robert Wagner in the title role while doing less than nothing for James as the Black Knight, unless you count the premiere at which he was allowed to sink his palm-prints into the concrete outside Grauman's Chinese Theatre in the hope of creating a little publicity. Beyond that, the film is now perhaps best remembered for a screenplay by Dudley Nichols which contained such gems as 'Father was right about those blasted Vikings', and James's courageous decision not to hide, as most of the rest of the cast were, behind several inches of beard.

By the time shooting on that was over, there was something very much more interesting on offer. For several months now, James had been hearing rumours that Judy Garland and her husband Sid Luft were at Warners to remake *A Star is Born,* one of the films that had always been central to the movie-making dream and its mythology. First shot in 1932 as *What Price Hollywood?* with Constance Bennett and Lowell Sherman, and then again in 1937 with Janet Gaynor and Fredric March, and most recently and catastrophically in 1976 with Barbra Streisand and Kris Kristofferson, its most famous and memorable version was the one that went into production in 1953 against considerable opposition, not least from Arthur Freed, the great master of movie musicals at MGM who, told that Luft and Garland were to be in charge of the production, memorably noted, 'those two alleycats can never make a picture'. This was a widely held view around Hollywood at that time: Garland, despite a recent concert comeback at the Palace on Broadway, was already reckoned to be hopelessly unreliable, and Luft inexperienced for what was now to be a wide-screen musical of considerable length and ambition. For this reason the role of the alcoholic star (thought to have been inspired by John Gilbert), whose career and life vanish into the Pacific Ocean just as his hitherto anonymous wife is inheriting his own stardom, had been turned down by just about everyone from Cary Grant to Humphrey Bogart by way of Brando, James Stewart and Montgomery Clift.

Eventually the Lufts got around to James, who leaped at it. Not only was the director to be one of the greatest, and the man who had made the very first version, George Cukor, but the score was by Harold Arlen and the screenplay was the work of one of America's most impressive playwrights and directors, Moss Hart. Except for *Julius Caesar,* this was far and away the most prestigious project that Mason had ever got or would ever get in California, and unlike

Caesar, which was always heavily theatrical, this one had the advantage of being pure film and pure Hollywood in its frame of reference.

Accordingly he lost little time in joining Garland on the Cukor set, and then spent much of the next three months fathering her through a difficult time, as Jane Greer recalls:

'If you saw them together on that *Star is Born* set, there was no doubt that Judy had fallen in love with James. She had slimmed down, done everything to make her performance work and was just desperate to please him.' For Amanda Blake, cast as Susan in the film, 'Judy was often very out of control, and certainly her husband who was producing could never control her, but James was always wonderful, very patient when she was late on the set, and used to do endless "driving shots" in the car so that the studio wouldn't realize how she was delaying the production. They were wonderful together, and James was so professional that he seemed to make up for Judy's unreliability; he kind of nursed her through it.'

Mason and Cukor did not get off to the easiest of starts, largely because Cukor wanted the part of Norman Maine played as a reflection of the late John Barrymore, and James wanted to go for something rather more personal to himself. It was, as Cukor said, 'Only in the end a matter of letting him find out things for himself: in that last scene, where he breaks down and decides to commit suicide, I just let the camera stay on him for a very long time and all his feelings came out.'

The final cut of the film ran to almost four hours, and it was then severely butchered by distributors all over America and Europe, so that the original full version did not surface again until an elaborate restoration job thirty years later. At that time, in 1984, Mason recalled for the *London Times* his memories of making *A Star is Born*:

'When I first arrived in Hollywood I had put myself at a very great disadvantage, because I didn't do any of the right things, so to be offered a film like this one was very special, even after it had been turned down by properly established people like Cary and Bogey. I had the greatest possible faith in Cukor and an admiration, a sort of love, for Judy who was marvellous to work with. Of course she had her difficulties; she'd got into this strange way of life when she was a kid at M G M, where the top brass wanted to get the most out of her so they didn't take it amiss if she took a little pick-me-up in the morning and sleeping pills at night. It became a habit with her, and of course in time got worse. On the set she didn't put in as many hours as a less talented woman would have done, but she was wonderfully easy; some mornings she couldn't start before eleven because of the pills, but once she was awake she was great – thoroughly professional, and a joy to work with. Sometimes she exasperated Cukor, but then he had to answer for her to Warners and the mood was not in favour of the picture. Judy hadn't made a film in the four years since MGM had dropped her from *Annie Get Your Gun*, and they never thought we'd finish this one, which is perhaps why they treated it so appallingly on first release, cutting it right back so they could squeeze in an extra afternoon showing in cinemas instead of just playing it twice a day.'

Though it didn't break any commercial records on its first outings, *A Star is Born* gradually became central to the Judy Garland story and was eventually recognized as her definitive screen musical of the postwar years; but for Mason, too, it was a considerable triumph. His portrait of the self-loathing, alcoholic actor living and eventually dying on the borderlines of a love-hate relationship with the motion picture industry drew deeply on his own ambiguous feelings about acting in general and Hollywood in particular, and despite the decision to reshoot whole sections of the picture in CinemaScope, which put the budget up from two to a record six million dollars, there was a wide expectation that both stars would be in line for the Oscars here. Indeed the only problem with James's performance, thought one critic, was that 'he endows Norman Maine with so sardonic a sense of humour and self-criticism that one cannot understand why a man of such intelligence should mind whether or not he continues to be a success in so hysterical and flimsy a place as Hollywood'.

In the event both were Oscar-nominated and then beaten, Judy by Grace Kelly in *A Country Girl* and James by Marlon Brando for *On The Waterfront*. He did, however, have the consolation of some of the best reviews of his entire career, and two hundred and fifty thousand dollars, his best salary yet though admittedly a reflection of the marathon twenty-two-week shooting schedule. Groucho Marx expressed the view that *A Star is Born*'s failure to take home star Oscars was 'the greatest robbery since Brink's'. From here, Garland was to start a slow run to the grave which she reached fifteen years later, as a result of what the coroner called 'an incautious self-dosage of a sleeping drug'. Her career had by then disintegrated into a series of increasingly tragic concert and television appearances, and she and James had lost touch after their one film together. Nevertheless it was James whom Liza Minnelli, Judy's daughter, asked to speak at Judy's funeral in New York:

'You close your eyes and you see a small, vivid woman, sometimes fat, sometimes thin, but vivid, vital ... I travelled in her orbit only for a while, but it was an exciting while, and one during which it seemed that the joys in her life outbalanced the miseries. The little girl whom I knew when she was good was not only very, very good but the most sympathetic, the funniest, the sharpest and the most stimulating woman I ever knew ... She gave so much and so richly that there was no currency in which to repay her: and she needed to be repaid, needed devotion and love beyond the resources of any of us ... Judy's gift was to wring tears from men with hearts of rock.'

23

'I now had a big house and should have been able to make a respectable income, at least until I chose to spend half the year acting in a tent in Canada.'

A *STAR IS BORN* at last managed to establish James as a stellar presence on the wide CinemaScope screen, and immediately after it came the offer from Walt Disney to play Captain Nemo in *20,000 Leagues Under The Sea*, the aquatic Jules Verne adventure which was up for the fourth of seven versions, putting James in a queue of Nemos, after Lionel Barrymore and Thomas Mitchell but ahead of Herbert Lom and Omar Sharif.

At first Mason resisted the offer, on the grounds that Disney was only really any good with animations or animals and that Kirk Douglas would anyway be getting top billing. Also, with elaborate underwater special effects, it was clearly going to be a producer's rather than an actor's film. But when the Disney offer rose to almost another quarter of a million dollars, plus a 'Portland clause' offering Mason's daughter the right to take home a print of any Disney movie she chose for the weekend (and this in a time way before videos), James decided he could no longer refuse.

His Captain Nemo was a creditable and efficient if rather routine performance, while *The Times* reckoned that 'his luxury submarine cabin, upholstered in red plush and fitted with cocktail bar, family organ, ornamental fountain and small but select gilt-tooled first editions, is in the best possible mixture of delightful and amusing

108

bad taste'. On the other hand that might just have been routine Hollywood set-dressing. Virginia Graham, for the *Spectator*, thought that James as usual 'broods with bitterness on the evils of men', and the director Richard Fleischer recalls:

'I always found James to be both abstract and abstracted: he was never really a Method actor but he was very internalized and on a film set he never seemed to feel it necessary to put other people at their ease. He just got on with his own work. Like most English actors he was a great technician, took a lot of trouble with accents, but he was one of the most honest performers I ever came across. He had no tricks, and once he had convinced himself that what he was doing in a scene was right, then he was just fine except on a day when by mistake we almost drowned him in a tank at Disney. Even that, though, was an experience he came through remarkably unperturbed: I guess the word for him was always "reserved".'

By now, however, Mason had decided on a major change of plan, one which was for the second time in his life to take him away from the studios where at last he had begun to build up a continuously successful career, and one from which it would again take him years to recover. This time James was leaving not a country but an industry: ever since the meetings with Gielgud on the set of *Julius Caesar*, he had been pondering the possibility of a return to the stage before the techniques that he had developed twenty years before got any more dried out under the California sun.

And with three major wide-screen pictures (*Caesar, Star* and the new Disney) under his belt, not to mention half a million dollars in the bank, this would surely be as good a moment as any to make that return to the theatre. The opportunity was not long in coming: a year earlier, in 1953, Mason's old director and mentor from the pre-war Old Vic, Tyrone Guthrie, had set up in a tent at Stratford, Ontario, a classical summer festival opening with a triumphant Alec Guinness/ Irene Worth season of *Richard III* and *All's Well That Ends Well*.

Now Guthrie was planning a second season, and again was in search of a star with some kind of classical theatrical background but also the ability to sell play tickets to Canadians who had as yet had little opportunity to become regular theatregoers. His eye fell swiftly on James, who was duly offered Angelo in *Measure For Measure* and the title role in *Oedipus Rex* for the summer of 1954, but almost no money at all.

109

Nevertheless Mason immediately accepted, much to the rage of Pamela who, having finally got her husband established as a true Hollywood movie star, saw little point in uprooting the family in his hour of triumph to go live in a small Canadian town several hours even from Toronto.

What James saw there was something very different: the chance to recapture his prewar days as a Guthrie actor, and perhaps at last to establish some kind of classical distinction on the other side of the Atlantic after years of usually minor Californian screenplays. But this was not going to be easily, if at all, achieved: Mason had done no live theatre since 1947, and no Shakespeare on stage since 1934, exactly twenty years earlier. By his own admission 'my range was limited, my speech colourless, my delivery casual. I had become a lazy cinema actor'.

For Frances Hyland, cast opposite James as Isabella in *Measure For Measure* and now one of Canada's most eminent actress-directors, Mason's arrival in Stratford, Ontario, was something of a revelation: 'First of all he drove across from California in a salmon-pink Ford convertible, which I don't think any of us in Ontario had ever seen before. Around Stratford the previous summer we got used to seeing Guinness on a bicycle. Then for a while he had Pamela and Portland staying, and they didn't care for it at all. When Guthrie did the *Oedipus* he had all the cast in classical masks, and Pamela said to James, "You've spent all these years trying to make your face famous all over the world and now you go and hide it behind a mask in Canada." She really couldn't understand what we were doing at all.

'Douglas Campbell, who was always one of the great resident stars out there, was also in the *Oedipus,* and he really had the voice for it; but what James had was a strange, silvery quality. He seemed even then to be a very ancient, quiet man with a terribly still centre. I think he was extremely brave to take on that season, given how little classical work he'd been doing since the war, but he always seemed such a lonely and melancholy man. Somehow he'd decided to make this great stage comeback and then found he just didn't have the theatrical strength for it, and it was really very sad to be with him while he was making that discovery. He was a kindly, gentle, generous, poetic gentleman, fascinated by the local Ontario church architecture: more fascinated by that than the theatre, I think, but

110

he felt he was somehow letting the side down and during the season he really did work very hard to get better. Yet by that time the reviews were in, and I think his pride had been rather hurt that they weren't nearly as good as they had been for Guinness in the opening season. With James you always felt there was more subtext than text, and a search for a happiness that he never quite managed to find. At least not in Canada.'

For Douglas Campbell, 'James was an extraordinarily intelligent and likable man, but I think he thought he was walking into a little summer-tent festival and it scared the pants off him when he discovered in rehearsal that he was working with some highly competent and experienced classicists. The real problem was that he seemed to have no voice, couldn't make himself heard, especially through those Guthrie masks for *Oedipus*, until later in the summer he found a voice coach and did some real work on his projection. But he remained very humble: in the next season I took over the *Oedipus* and he sent me a first-night cable reading "Now at last it will be played properly".

'He also wasn't helped by Pamela and Portland being so bored and not understanding the life there, and I don't think they shared his love for the theatre at all. That very smoky voice which was so wonderful and distinctive on a film soundtrack was really terrible in a theatre, because it had no depth or variety. His Angelo and his Oedipus were very intelligent readings of the roles, but they were postage-stamp size and they didn't really get anywhere. I think he suddenly realized in rehearsal that he'd bitten off more than he could chew, and that he'd left it too late to get back to a theatre life. He was desperately ready to learn and take advice, but somehow the energy just wasn't there.'

Reviews were by no means terrible, but they damned Mason with a faint kind of praise, noting that he seemed 'overawed' by the plays. On his last night, however, there were cheers for the *Oedipus*, and it was left to Herbert Whittaker of the Toronto *Globe & Mail* to sum up: 'This has been a very difficult time for the successful film actor. He has ventured back to the stage after many years' absence from it, and to a very strange stage indeed. He has tackled two difficult roles, one which deprived him of his stock-in-trade, the famous face, and made ferocious demands on his equally famous voice when he accepted its ancient convention of masks. But James

Mason did not fail as a man at Stratford: his untiring effort to improve his performances, his unfailing simplicity and sympathy, won him a very firm friendship with the entire company of his fellow actors.'

Nevertheless, in the remaining thirty years of his life Mason was only to make three more stage appearances, and all of those in contemporary work. It was at Stratford that he bade a long farewell to any hopes he might still have cherished of becoming a classical actor, or indeed a stage actor of any lasting integrity or fame.

24

'The actor who never mixes movie acting with stage acting is the one to feel sorry for, and he is generally in Hollywood where it is impossible to find out whether he is really any good or not.'

BACK IN LOS ANGELES from the Canadian adventure late in 1954, James was once again plunged into deep gloom about his life and his career. Domestically things had turned rough in Stratford with Pamela's insistence that he was wasting his time back on the boards, and when he did return to Hollywood it was to discover that, despite a run of success in *Caesar*, *A Star is Born* and *20,000 Leagues*, there now seemed to be no demand whatsoever for his services on film.

Always one of the most observant and intelligent of the Hollywood English, James realized that he had returned at a time of considerable change: those of his generation who had relied on the old officers-and-gentlemen image, men like Edmund Purdom and Peter Lawford, were having to lose their Sandhurst accents and acquire something more acceptably mid-Atlantic, while the very reason that had brought most of them to Hollywood after the war had ceased to exist. If epics like *Quo Vadis* could now be made with Californian money, but in Rome or Madrid, there was really not much point in a Beverly Hills address. Even a writer like Christopher Fry, who twenty years earlier would have been obliged to follow Walpole and Sherriff out to Hollywood, was able in the 1950s to write biblical epics without ever crossing the Atlantic, and David Lean was already

113

among the first great directors to steer clear of any American studio cities.

Moreover, the most successful of the California British had ceased to be particularly or noticeably British at all. In postwar films, Cary Grant and Elizabeth Taylor as often as not played American, while one of the most triumphant of all the Hollywood Raj in terms of longevity and commercial profit virtually never appeared on screen as anything but American: Bob Hope.

Back home, the generation of movie stars just below Mason's, the generation of John Mills and Richard Attenborough and Trevor Howard, were all managing to have international careers without ever losing an English work-base, while in America another whole generation of actors like Paul Newman and Marlon Brando were returning the American industry to its native roots. Mason now suddenly and unhappily realized that he had lost his place in the pantheon that ran from Olivier and Gielgud through Redgrave and Richardson to Guinness and Scofield, by giving up both his theatre and his country at precisely the wrong moment. He took refuge once again in some rather bitter journalism.

'I became acutely conscious when I was in Britain recently that I had missed an awful lot by specializing in movies. My contemporaries who stayed in the British theatre had become robust, resourceful stars basking nightly in the glow of audience approval, a comfort not extended to movie actors. It is a life-giving glow: it stimulates an actor's inventiveness and gives him courage, it intoxicates and liberates ... In London it is not difficult for the actor to enjoy the best of both worlds. The drive to the theatre in the West End or the movie studio in the suburbs is equally convenient. An actor can alternate the one with the other. He can specialize in the live theatre and fit a movie into his programme when pressed for money to meet his income tax demands. Or he can specialize in movies and take a theatre engagement whenever he begins to feel unloved. For the actor in New York, things are not quite so good. If he wants to make a movie he has to travel three thousand miles to a place he affects to despise. And his life in the live Broadway theatre is much more of a gamble than it is anywhere else in the theatrical world ... Meanwhile in Hollywood the good are no good unless they are successful, and the successful are scared and mistrustful of an achievement for which they cannot confidently take much of the credit ... I apologize for writing the biography of such a fellow, for that is primarily what I am.'

The rest of the 1950s were passed in a haze of aborted producing projects and inadequate movies, until Hitchcock rescued him at the very end of the decade for *North by Northwest* – though even there only to play the heavy opposite Cary Grant's suave Rushmore-climbing hero. In the meantime, and in the absence of any film offers on his return from Stratford, Mason solemnly announced his total retirement from the big screen. At the age of forty-five he would, he said, be turning towards production, though before that he was not averse to accepting £1,500 a week for hosting a curiously disastrous live television series called 'The Lux Video Theatre'. James's role was to link the dramas with the commercials, one he performed with obvious embarrassment at being caught up in something so fundamentally unsuited to his character and temperament. He and Pamela also announced to a somewhat aghast world that they would soon be producing 'a series of Biblical and historical television films in colour to star Portland', who was then all of six and a half but the subject of considerable gossip-column attention largely because she seemed to be the oldest child of her age even in Beverly Hills.

Eventually a film did come along, albeit one that James often afterwards wished had not: *Forever Darling* was, in 1955, the first time Mason played a guardian angel on screen, followed twenty-two years later by his second, in Warren Beatty's rather more satisfactory *Heaven Can Wait*. This first one did at least unite James with one of his greatest heroines, the comedienne Lucille Ball, but in a screenplay of such stunning awfulness that, as one critic noted, 'It is to be hoped that they paid Mr Mason handsomely for aiding and abetting this disaster, because he is going to be a long time living it down'.

In fact his money had already slumped from its *Star is Born* peak, and James was now mainly making news for a series of increasingly spectacular lawsuits, all of which were ultimately settled out of court. First there was a fan magazine suggesting again that his marriage was on the rocks; then a scandal-sheet called *Rave* accused him of 'immoral conduct' and got hit for a million dollars; and finally a television writer accused him of having been 'disloyal to England' by not fighting the war, and was sued for three million.

'People in California,' James told me more in sorrow than in anger years later, 'were always trying to find something wrong with me, but the only things they had to draw on were that Pamela's ex-husband lived over our garage, and that I liked a lot of cats. So then they had to invent things, and I used to wait to see what new scandal I was involved in. Invariably it began 'ménage à trois', though after the papers got bored of that they started to focus on Portland. My wife once cut the pocket off an old mink coat and let Portland take it to bed, so overnight she became the only child in Hollywood with her own mink. Then once we sneaked her into Ciro's so they announced she was forever in nightclubs. It was as though the English press wanted to know that we'd all somehow gone to seed by living in wicked America.'

As often in times of professional crisis, James now began to get increasingly wrapped up in a private dream: to become a producer of good movies rather than continue as an actor in bad ones. Twentieth Century Fox offered him a contract which would allow that, and after playing around for a while with Richard Hughes's *A High Wind in Jamaica,* which proved ultimately unacceptable to the Zanuck power-brokers around the studio, James spent the next few months at work on an ambitious project to re-make *Jane Eyre* with himself as Mr Rochester and the then unknown Joanne Woodward in the title role. But that proved altogether too risky a prospect for Fox, and after sending a script to Audrey Hepburn, who rejected it, they reassigned an embittered but embattled James to a different film in which he had also expressed an interest.

This was *Bigger Than Life,* an honourable disaster but one so total (at any rate in box-office terms) as to kill almost all of the dreams James had left of a career behind the camera, or one which would in any way allow him to control his own destiny as an actor. Based on a medical report in the *New Yorker,* the film told the quasi-documentary story of an amiable American schoolteacher driven by overdoses of cortisone to attempt the killing of his entire family, and it had the distinction of Nicholas Ray as director and Clifford Odets as screenwriter.

It was not, however, the kind of story American audiences were then accustomed to in colour on the wide screen, and though it attracted immensely respectful reviews from Godard and Truffaut in the French *Cahiers du Cinema,* and a gala showing at the Venice Film Festival, on American and English release it attracted dis-

116

missive reviews and hysterical denials from the drug industry, but no audiences.

During James's production year at Fox, Pamela had given birth to a second child: Morgan was, like Portland, also to make occasional appearances in his father's films but neither child maintained an acting career as an adult. Portland took, in later life, to writing poetry, while Morgan went into rock music and then a publicity and personal-management career by way of the White House, where he worked as a public relations aide to the Reagans during the Bloomingdale scandal. It was Morgan who once, talking to his father, summarized what he saw as their essential problem: 'While Portland has a lot of talent but no ambition, I have ambition but no talent.'

25

'North By Northwest *was the last of the Hitchcock classics,*
typical in that the form was everything and the content
nonexistent.'

LOOKING BACK ON his abortive and unhappy time as a producer at
Fox, James reckoned he should have taken the advice of Nunnally
Johnson and 'just had a good time in my office reading books
and writing letters and giving interviews'; unfortunately he had
decided the job also involved making movies, and the only one he'd
achieved, *Bigger Than Life,* was now showing up in red on the
studio accounts. They still had one film left on the contract, but
Zanuck made it clear this was to involve Mason purely as an actor:
Island in the Sun was based on a novel by Evelyn Waugh's brother,
Alec, which, whatever its original virtues, had been reduced by
the screenplay to what one critic called 'washed out anti-black male
sexuality'.

It was in fact a kind of inter-racial soap opera in one long episode,
best remembered for Harry Belafonte singing the title song and
having an affair with Joan Fontaine while another white, John Justin,
had an affair with the black Dorothy Dandridge, watched from the
sidelines by a pre-Dynastic Joan Collins worrying about her own
bloodlines, and by James as a murderously neurotic Jamaican plan-
tation-owner. Sir Hugh Foot, then governor of Jamaica, took to the
Observer's correspondence columns to complain that the film was
'thoroughly offensive' in its obsession with miscegenation, and most

other critics around the world just reckoned that it really wasn't very good.

Not only had Mason's film career reached rock bottom by the late 1950s: his marriage to Pamela had failed to strengthen as a result of Morgan's birth, and there were now real signs of a rift. Diana de Rosso recalls:

'The whole atmosphere was that of people leading totally separate lives within the same large household; it all seemed amicable enough, but there was no sense of a couple who wanted to be together. James appeared to be in limbo, living in a house that certainly wasn't really his home. I think he was devoted to the children, but unlike Pam he was terribly slow in deciding whether or not to take American citizenship – something, in fact, he never did. He remained oddly foreign and alone out there. You always sensed that he wanted to return to England, although I don't think he thought there would be much of a life for him at home either. Certainly his Yorkshire family didn't go out of their way to urge him back, and I think he came to accept that his children would end up as Americans, although he was always very critical of what people called the American dream. He wanted something quieter and more academic which just didn't seem to exist out there, and he had a very low boredom threshold.

'James was never as cold or unemotional as he looked, but he found it terribly hard to accept an American way of life with his Yorkshire upbringing. He was a very complex, uneasy man and towards the end of his Hollywood life he looked as if he was just sleepwalking, waiting for something or someone to come along and wake him up out of a self-imposed trance. But at the moment when his career was in real trouble, at the end of the 1950s, when they were telling him that he had no power to sell tickets around America, he suddenly discovered just how ambitious he really was. He had never wanted to be a star when he first became one, in England during the war; now that he was slipping in California, he suddenly desperately wanted to get it all back, and no longer had the scripts which would allow him to do it. That really was a very disappointing and sad time for him, and I think he thought if he woke up one more morning and saw that bloody sun and the palm trees he would go mad. But he wouldn't discuss the possibility of ending the marriage or going back to Europe. He just sublimated the whole thing under that usual, impassive façade.'

The films that came along now, in 1958, were no longer from any major studio. Instead, there were a couple of low-budget thrillers called *Cry Terror* and *The Decks Ran Red,* put together by the independent producer Andrew L. Stone.

'We used to lunch together about once a week', Stone remembers, 'and I had the impression of a very unhappy man, but what I liked about him was that he wasn't one of those phony Englishmen like Niven, who created a character for himself as that cheery soldier. Mason was totally sincere, a little tight-fisted with the tips maybe, but you always knew where you stood with him and he would never let you down. The pictures we made together could maybe have been a bit better, but we were very pressed for time and James was always there on cue, always professional.'

The first of these Stone thrillers cast James as a television repair-man held hostage by a manic plane-bomber, Rod Steiger:

'There was something oddly tragic about Mr Mason. You felt that things in his life were eating away at him, and that he was always in a tremendous kind of emotional pain which he was bravely trying to hide. So the façade was always there, and he seemed to take pride in putting up a front as though everything was all right, when you knew that deep down it couldn't possibly be. He was a great technician, and it may have been that, like me, he got too far away from the theatre where we both spent the first decade of our careers, and then could never get back in touch with it. But there was something churning inside of him, and although he never let it show in his work, you could always sense it. He was a tenacious son of a bitch, and a great survivor, but I think he was maybe too intelligent for some of the work he had to do in movies.'

The second Stone thriller, *The Decks Ran Red,* found James as an inexperienced ship's captain facing mutiny and mass-murder on a maiden voyage. His co-star was Stuart Whitman, who says now: 'Likable, quiet man, very low-key and always seemed to be reading. Kept his distance from the cast and the crew, but never exactly unfriendly, just somehow very reserved around people he hadn't known for too long.'

Both films met with a hail of abuse from English critics, and it was with a kind of relief that Mason then turned briefly back to the theatre, not risking anything as exposed as Broadway or the West End but instead doing a couple of summer-stock seasons in light comedies at La Jolla, California, and Ivorytown, Connecticut.

These were in fact his penultimate stage appearances, and another twenty years were to elapse before he would make one last assault on Broadway. Meantime, back in Beverly Hills, there followed yet another legal battle, this one with the tabloid press. Mason had been approached by the BBC in London with a view to making thirty-nine half-hour television thrillers as Harry Lime, the character created by Orson Welles in *The Third Man* and eventually recreated for the series by Michael Rennie. When the Mason negotiations broke down, partly because of the money offered and partly because James was, even at this nadir of his film career, still uneasy about relegating himself to what was then regarded as an actors' graveyard in television, two national tabloids in England ran stories to the effect that he had insisted on a 'war clause' stating that in the event of any hostilities breaking out in Europe he could in no way be eligible for military service. As James was now well into his fiftieth year, this would have been a little unlikely anyway, but stung by what seemed a deliberate attempt to hark back to his wartime pacifism and the disputes it provoked, Mason sued for three and a half million dollars in damages and eventually settled for a sizable out-of-court payment which he gave to charity.

In Hollywood things at last started to improve briefly as, and some would say not before time, Mason at last came to the attention of Alfred Hitchcock. James might have made a perfect hero for almost any of Hitchcock's major postwar thrillers: suave and faintly sinister, honourable and yet somehow suspicious, he could have brought distinction and dramatic intensity to the roles played by James Stewart or Cary Grant through the 1950s. But by that time Hitchcock had his casting priorities firmly set, and it was still a widely held Hollywood belief that James's name above a title did not sell tickets in the all-important Midwest. He merely guaranteed slightly better reviews in the upmarket big-city papers at home and abroad, especially in France where he was always regarded by the *Cahiers du Cinema* crowd as a more intriguing actor than most.

Thus for *North By Northwest*, Hitchcock offered him not the Cary Grant role of the innocent advertising executive mistaken for a spy and almost crop-dusted to death, but that of the elegant and faintly bisexual espionage chief who spends most of the picture trying unsuccessfully to get Grant wiped off the face of the earth.

James duly turned in a masterly villain – as polished and heavy as a Kremlin banister, thought the *New York Times* – and it is arguable that in all of Hitchcock there is no smoother killer, nor one in whom there was patently so much more going on beneath the surface, despite the director's usual technical interest in form rather than content. Mason's performance also had an element of wry self-mockery which has been plundered by actors playing master villains in hundreds, if not thousands of television movies over the intervening thirty years. As so often in his career, the credit has seldom been given him for it.

But with Cary Grant now an almost totally reclusive if wealthy figure (at a million dollars each, he and Hitch were getting roughly ten times the salary granted to James), and Hitchcock himself equally unapproachable off the set, the *North By Northwest* locations would have been a lonely time for Mason had he not happened to meet a Chicago publicist and ex-Munchkin from *The Wizard of Oz*, Donna Greenberg, who was to become an increasingly important and central part of James's life as his marriage to Pamela crumbled further towards a divorce.

26

'The only way I stayed the course was through sheer pig-headedness: after that succession of really terrible Hollywood films, most self-respecting actors would have packed their bags and fled years before I did.'

'IT WAS A little sad,' says the actor Martin Landau who played Mason's sidekick in *North By Northwest,* 'seeing him on that film playing second string to Cary Grant when he himself had been a star of so many others. Hitchcock had worked with Grant a lot, and so they were naturally close, whereas I think James felt rather left out and suddenly realized that he'd reached some kind of turning point. At fifty he was now playing the character man, no longer the leading role, and although he would hardly ever talk about something so personal as that, you could sense that it hurt and made him even more guarded. He seemed very worried about his voice, which he always thought very nasal and self-limiting; he always said he envied the poetry in Burton or Gielgud, and that he could never match their musicality and range. There was an odd mixture of loneliness and yet a desperate desire for friendship about him, as though he wanted to be alone a lot and somehow couldn't quite bear it when he was.'

With a rapidly disintegrating marriage, but a wife and two young children still to support in a large California house, Mason went straight from *North By Northwest* into *Journey To The Centre of the Earth,* another Jules Verne adventure with which Twentieth Century Fox hoped he might repeat his *20,000 Leagues* success. His

123

co-star on this occasion was the actress Arlene Dahl.

'We spent about three months on location in Mexican caverns,' she recalls, 'and in that time I came to realize that although he was extremely crusty on the outside, James was soft as a marshmallow at his centre. I always thought he seemed an unhappy man who found a kind of consolation in the work when it was going well, but he was very private about that, too. I remember his fury later in Hollywood when work had to stop and we were all summoned to meet Mr Krushchev who was on some sort of state visit to the studios. James couldn't bear the idea of being polite to him just because he was a world leader. I think he had a deep distrust of almost all politicians. There was a kind of sadness in his eyes which only disappeared at the very end of his life, when he was into his second marriage, and although quite rightly he had great confidence in himself as an actor, he didn't seem to have much of it in himself as a man.'

For Pat Boone, also cast in that film, the irony was that 'here was this great actor doing a picture for which I as a pop singer was getting vastly better paid, because I really only wanted to do musicals; so in order to get me into this one they had to give me a sizable percentage of the gross, and I know he wasn't getting anything like that. It was also a little embarrassing that I was in the box-office top ten at that time and he was nowhere near it, but he was professional enough never to let any of his discontent show through. This was evidently not going to be a milestone in his or anyone's career, but it was a job he needed so he just got on with it as professionally as possible, and I think that was very typical of the man. Certainly one never had the impression of a very happy or contented figure, but there was a definite pride in the work that shone through.'

With little to keep him in California either professionally or privately, James took up an invitation from Ivan Foxwell, the British producer, who in Mason's words 'opened a window in my coop and reintroduced me to the sunshine and the fresh air'. Hollywood had become a prison, yet back in Scotland, on location for *A Touch of Larceny,* James was rediscovering not only a love of his own territories (he had revisited his family in Yorkshire on the way north, for the first time in several years) but also a long-buried talent for light comedy. The film told of an Admiralty officer posing for romantic reasons as a Russian spy, and although modestly made on a low budget, Guy Hamilton's direction served as none other had in the last decade to rehabilitate James in the eyes of British movie critics. 'Mason's performance,' wrote the *Evening Standard*, 'bland and wryly humorous, pursues its objectives with the tenacity of a homing torpedo; his portrayal indicates that we may see more of Mason sweet rather than Mason sour, and without recourse to either bedroom or deadpan humour, the film restores to British screen comedy something that has been missing since Ealing days.'

It also led to a close friendship with the Hitchcock actress Vera Miles, and a sense that somehow, away from Hollywood which had proved so emotionally and cinematically arid of late, James was now enjoying something of a rebirth on screen as well as off. Another critic highlighted the change: 'We see Mason here with new eyes, a light comedian of the top rank, wiping out those dull Hollywood years and variations on *The Man in Grey*.'

For the producer Ivan Foxwell, who made both *A Touch of Larceny* and *Tiara Tahiti* with James, he was a man in search of a new screen identity: 'In California soon after the war I'd seen James taking part in amateur theatricals, playing in Victorian melodramas just for friends, and I suddenly realized what a marvellous light comedian he would be. The studio wanted me to get Niven for *A Touch of Larceny*, and he would have been the more commercial casting, but I knew that James could deliver something altogether more interesting and detailed.

'When I first saw the Masons in California, Kellino was still around and there was that curious uncertainty which none of us in those days dared to ask very much about, especially with Pamela who was kind of formidable. I don't think James was at all bisexual, but I do think he had a very low sex drive which probably explained a lot. He was also still very hung up on his refusal to fight the war, which I never really understood, and there was an odd mix of courage and guilt there.

'Undoubtedly James's private life was very jumbled up: he wasn't a weak man but Pamela was a very strong lady, and I think he felt the need to live up to her original wealth and the power of her family in a way he found ultimately impossible. During *A Touch of Larceny* he became devoted to Vera Miles, but I don't think anything much came of that: there was always a rather wistful, unrealized quality to James's romantic attachments.

'I saw that instead of the usual villains he played there was a much funnier and more complex actor there, and by the time I began to work with James he was already terribly disillusioned by California and desperate to get back to Europe. He only really stayed there because Pamela and the children seemed to love it, but he always appeared both unhappy and unrealized in Hollywood. *Larceny* brought him back to Britain for the first time in ages, and I think that may have been the turning point, when he knew he couldn't stay abroad forever.

'He was a shy, wry man, eager to be loved but somehow still so reserved that it was difficult to get through to him even on a long location like this one up in Scotland. His career and his life in California were in fact breaking up, but he would never refer to that except obliquely. George Sanders was also in the film and in some ways not unlike him, though lacking James's ultimate profession-alism. Later, when we came to do *Tiara Tahiti* with John Mills, there were terrible rows about billing, and I suddenly realized how much James's stardom meant to him and how terrified he was of slipping in to the role of just a "charactor actor", though in fact much of his best work was done towards the end of his life. I think he was the finest screen actor I ever met, and even when he had to pay for the Pam divorce by making a lot of rubbish he still was capable of giving these haunting performances. Towards the end of his life we would occasionally meet for lunch or dinner and there was something infinitely sad about his awareness that he was no longer quite the star he had once been: a vastly intelligent man, he could never easily come to terms with the whims of the film industry over the years. He was really too bright to deal with Hollywood. Where Niven was a natural star but not a very good actor, James was the reverse. Unlike Niven he wasn't terribly sexy, and I think the camera can recognize a kind of private coldness, a low degree of sexuality and a rather cynical, almost academic interest in women. There was a remarkable kind of distance there: every time he started a film he would check his own performance in the first day's rushes and then never go near the screenings again. I think he was like that about people, too, unless he felt he could really trust them. He was never quite a rebel, but nor did he ever fit in easily anywhere.'

Mason stayed in England to narrate a short documentary about the history of Big Ben and then to make one more film, the Peter

Finch version of the life and trials of Oscar Wilde. This was shot as wide-screen technicolor competition for a black-and-white version of the same story starring Robert Morley. While James played Carson, the prosecuting counsel responsible for Wilde's arrest on charges of homosexuality, the same role was played in the Morley version by Sir Ralph Richardson. It was an unfair contest, given Sir Ralph's altogether superior stage and screen manner, and the most that can be said of it is that James came a good second.

He then returned to the Buster Keaton house in Beverly Hills, which now stood on Pamela Drive, a geographic location she had managed to inaugurate by subdividing the land. The few months he had spent in Scotland and Yorkshire and around London studios had indicated to James that as Britain moved into the 1960s, it was becoming an altogether more desirable place to live and work than when he had left it fifteen years earlier. Moreover, with the collapse of the old Hollywood studios, the coming of international jet travel and the multinational movie, there was really nothing to keep Mason in California except two children at school there and a wife who showed no desire or inclination to leave.

For their sake, however, he spent another couple of years trying with increasing difficulty to come to terms with the life, and even went straight from *The Trials of Oscar Wilde* into another really terrible Hollywood movie for Fox. *The Marriage-Go-Round* had been a Broadway hit for Charles Boyer and Claudette Colbert as a couple of college professors in marital trouble, but as *Time* uncharitably noted 'instead of them we now have James Mason, an actor who could not crack a joke if it was a lichee nut, and Susan Hayward, a bargain-basement Bette Davis whose lightest touch as a comedienne would stun a horse'. Whatever James had learned about comedy for *A Touch of Larceny* seems to have deserted him once he got back to the gloom of his Californian life.

By now the household on Pamela Drive was getting to be very difficult indeed for James: their faithful Irish retainer John Monaghan was still around, but Roy Kellino had gone off to a new marriage and then an all-too-early death, and James himself was now seeing more and more of Donna Greenberg:

'I had the impression of this deeply unhappy man with a marriage in real trouble for all kinds of reasons on both sides, though I guess

127

I was the final trigger of the divorce a couple of years later when Pamela found out about us. After we'd first met in Chicago on *North By Northwest* I'd moved out to California with my little son, and James and I began travelling together on his film locations and seeing a lot of each other. We went to Tahiti and Spain, and even had plans to marry for a while after his divorce came through, but that took a very long time and in the end I'd married someone else. James was the handsomest man I ever saw and the most wonderful, gentle and intelligent teacher and yet very non-judgmental, and I loved him very much. He showed me how to like books and music, and although he was going through some very painful emotional times at home, and eventually came out with the most terrible skin rash, he was always wonderful to me, always had time to listen to my troubles though he had more than enough of his own, especially as he was so torn about the children.

'He desperately wanted to get away from Pamela and California, but he didn't want to leave Portland and Morgan behind. He was terrified that Pamela would get custody of them and they'd become totally American children and be lost to the kind of European life which he now wanted to get back to. He always said to me that he felt like a foreigner in America and even more of a foreigner in his own home. Although he was still doing those wonderful line drawings of the cats and the children, he was heartbroken about the way that his family ties had gone wrong in the generations both side of him, so that he couldn't really get close to his parents or his children because of the way his own life had worked out. He once told me that his father had said there were only three things he didn't want his sons to be; a preacher, a teacher and an actor, and he got all three.

'James had this very repressed English childhood and it left him all his life unable to express emotions very coherently; but he used to show me photographs of his Yorkshire home and more and more he seemed to want out of America. When he was working back in England he would take me to places he'd loved, and he seemed somehow so much brighter and happier than when he was trying to sort out his marriage and his career and his life in California, especially when he realized that there wasn't much of any of that left. I always felt safer with him than with anyone else, though towards the end of his life we drifted apart after he married again, and the last time we met was on a pavement in Beverly Hills and I suddenly saw in his eyes that he couldn't remember me at all, though clearly by then he was really quite ill. I think he was probably the greatest film actor ever: his tragedy was to be that in a Hollywood where they really only respected movie stars.'

27

'Lolita *was one of my best adventures in film-making, and it also marked the end of one period of my life and the beginning of another: it took me to England for a longer period than usual, and when it was over I felt that a repatriation had taken place and that I no longer lived in California.'*

MASON CONTINUED FOR a while to go through the motions of life in Beverly Hills. He even made one last family film for Portland Productions, *Hero's Island*, which he co-produced with the writer–director Leslie Stevens. James played the seventeenth-century pirate Blackbeard and there was a sizable role for Morgan, who later went on to play Elizabeth Taylor's child in *The Sandpiper*. He then abandoned an acting career, much as Portland would after a teenage appearance in one of the *St Trinian's* screen adventures.

One of the other characters in the film was a fisherman called Enoch Gates, and in his desperation to find some sort of new start to his Californian life Mason for a while quite seriously took on the persona of an ancient character actor of that name, appearing uncredited in minor roles for television westerns and wondering whether, as old Enoch, he might be able to live out his later years buried way down supporting-cast lists.

Abandoning that notion as impractical even by his standards, James now turned to an equally radical alternative: noting that Rex Harrison had recently managed to revive a flagging but not altogether dissimilar career by singing and dancing on stage in *My Fair Lady*, Mason began seriously to consider the possibilities of a return to the New York stage in a new Dietz and Schwartz musical based on

Schnitzler's *Affairs of Anatol*. Indeed, so far had he got with preparations for this, including his first-ever singing and dancing lessons, that his instinct was to refuse the next film that came along.

Fortunately he had second thoughts, for the film was *Lolita*. By now, early in 1961, the role of the middle-aged university lecturer who falls in love with a girl of twelve had been rejected by, among others, David Niven, Rex Harrison and Noël Coward, all of whom felt it was more than a little risky at best and at worst likely to be totally destructive of any public image they had managed to establish in the minds of an audience. Ever the rebel outsider in a situation like that, Mason decided that the challenge was worth it, though he did draw the line at suggestions that Portland be cast in the title role.

That, in the event, went to Sue Lyon, but the picture itself went to Peter Sellers as Quilty, the degenerate playwright who steals the girl and the film. 'I remember James,' says his early love, Ann Todd, of this period in his life, 'coming away from the studios deeply depressed that he'd taken the wrong part and that Sellers in the flashier role was going to get all the notices.' Which was exactly what happened: *Time* magazine even suggested that it was Sellers who should have played Humbert, adding that 'Mason behaves like an Englishman who has been caught cheating at cards at his club, while showing none of the Old World graces and cultural refinement that made the book's Humbert seem more of a sexual gourmet than a sexual monster'.

Others were more enthusiastic: Alexander Walker for the *Standard*, after describing 'another Sellers triumph', wrote of a 'stimulating and entertaining and cautionary tale', and Kubrick himself reckoned he'd never have found better casting than Mason, an opinion endorsed for the *New Yorker* by Pauline Kael: 'His Humbert makes attractiveness tired and exhausted and impotent, and he is better than anyone could have expected... Mason's career has been so mottled: a beautiful *Odd Man Out*, a dull Brutus, an uneven but often brilliant Normain Maine in *A Star is Born*, a good Captain Nemo and then in 1960 the beginnings of a comic style in *A Touch of Larceny* as that handsome face gloats in a rotting smile'.

Sellers may have stolen *Lolita* from Mason, just as he was about to steal the *Pink Panther* series from its original star David Niven, but there could be no doubt that the debate over the Nabokov—

Kubrick picture and its brilliance or immorality, one which continued for many months in both highbrow and popular papers on both sides of the Atlantic, put James's career back onto a serious critical level for the first time in a decade or more. Even before the shooting started, he immersed himself so deeply in the role that one very close friend remembers him coming off the plane from Los Angeles 'not as himself at all, but already as Humbert'. That was an impression confirmed by Shelley Winters, who played Lolita's mother:

'He had a curious ability to become the men he played, so that all through the shooting he remained in character, but there was a constant reservoir of anguish when you got to know him privately. Ralph Richardson once told me James was one of the greatest actors in the world, but I don't think he ever quite believed it himself. He always behaved as if there was some terrible secret in his past, whereas I think it was just that he'd always been unhappy. In a way one almost expected him to be Irish: there was all that poetic melancholy inside him.'

From *Lolita*, James turned to something much lighter: after pausing briefly for an uncredited guest shot as a garage mechanic in his old friend Ronald Neame's *Escape from Zahrein* he went to the South Seas for another of Ivan Foxwell's maritime comedy adventures, one that cast him in an odd-couple team with John Mills as a pair of wartime ex-soldiers fighting a class battle with each other in *Tiara Tahiti*. For Ted Kotcheff, a television director on his first wide-screen assignment, 'James was an enormous help and wonderful to work with once you got over a terrible shyness. At the beginning of dinner every night on the location there would be these long anguished pauses. Then gradually he would open up and start talking about his life and the women he'd known and the mistakes he'd made, so that by the end of the night you really thought you'd broken through his reserve, but the next evening the long pauses would be there and you'd have to start all over again, as though you'd never met. He was always the first one on the set in the morning, murmuring his lines to himself, and utterly dedicated to his craft but whenever he talked about his childhood, or his own children, there was a neurotic kind of humour as though he thought he'd come from some very odd sort of background. He was a civilized, cultured, compassionate man, and what you saw on the screen was what you got in real life. There was no kind of created image. Working with him all those years later, I remembered that I'd seen his *Oedipus* in Stratford, Ontario, and the performance suddenly came back to haunt me. At the time it was dismissed locally as the work of a cinema actor who couldn't cope with the stage, but in retrospect I think it was much better than that.

'A couple of times I went to dinner with him in that Buster Keaton house in Hollywood where they'd found some old films of his behind a secret panel; the marriage was very rocky, but James just sat there taking it, almost as though he was really someplace quite different in his mind. He was always enchanted by women, not a man's man at all but terribly romantic, kept falling in love with the Tahitians but in a very idealistic sort of way. Pamela was a very ballsy, modern, emancipated kind of woman and I think he was by now looking for someone rather more old-fashioned and feminine, but he was always very abstracted. Somewhere inside himself I believe he thought he was not quite in the first rank of actors, because the English have always had that belief about the stage coming first, whereas in America they accept the greatness of movie stars like Bogart or Spencer Tracy. In the English scheme of things James knew he was never going to be Richardson or Redgrave or Gielgud or Olivier, and I think that faintly depressed him, even though he always said he had no desire to go back to a theatrical life.'

Sir John Mills, looking back on James in *Tiara Tahiti*, recalled 'a splendid actor, shy, charming but somehow rather sad. I felt he would have been happier if he'd resisted the call of Hollywood, which he apparently didn't much like.'

By the time *Tiara Tahiti* was in the can, and James had returned to live in California for the last time, news that his marriage to Pamela was drawing somewhat unpeacefully to a close had begun to reach local gossip columnists. Mason announced in characteristically clenched fashion that his marriage was now in 'a slightly critical situation' and then expanded: 'This is no sudden decision, but it is of course very sad. You'd better put it down to differences in tastes and aspirations. My wife had no misgivings about taking out American citizenship because she felt American: she succeeded where I failed in becoming a wholehearted member of that community. The children are also likely to stay here, where Portland already has an acting career, but I would like to settle back in England and see more of my parents. Looking back, I see I would have done much better to stay in England rather than spend these fourteen years in Hollywood. My first five pictures were ghastly flops and the situation worsened when CinemaScope brought in a passion for big, flashy spectaculars. The only interesting work I've ever had has been in eccentric low-budget movies or television, and I ever didn't go out to Hollywood for that.

'Here in Europe now they have come to depend less and less on star value and more and more on the merits of the actual picture, and for that reason the work is just so much better'.

Pamela, meanwhile, was giving her own interviews, not just to local journalists but on the radio and television chat shows where she was carving out her own career as a talkative hostess:

'James is a strange man, you know, very moody. One night when we had some guests he just got up from the table, poured himself a glass of prune juice and went to bed, turning off all the lights, totally forgetting there was anyone else in the room. He just tuned us all out, so you can see it wasn't the easiest of marriages. I think actors are unbearable children, living in a world of their own and constantly talking about themselves. I really don't like them very much.'

After twenty-one years, the Mason marriage reached a Santa Monica divorce court with Pamela suing James for 'habitual adultery', a charge which somewhat shocked her half-sister Diana:

'There were faults on both sides, as in many marriages. The divorce was the best thing they could have done by then. James was desperately worried that the children would be contaminated by the greed of the American dream, and he felt that if he could stay in touch with them then he would be able to have some sort of influence over them, which was why he allowed Pamela to make it such a one-sided battle. In the end he would just give into everything her lawyers demanded, I think, because all he really wanted for himself was an escape back to Europe.'

28

'To be a successful film star as opposed to a successful film actor, you should settle for an image and polish it forever: I somehow could never quite bring myself to do that.'

As HE PREPARED to pack up a Californian life that had lasted fifteen years, and at the age of fifty-four return to start a new career with nothing but the need to find five hundred pounds a week maintenance for Pamela, Mason seemed understandably more depressed than usual. 'I suppose every man has a grand idea of self-fulfilment which inevitably he then falls short of; the art is just to go on, even after you realize the shortcomings.'

But with what? He was, he reckoned, too old and in need of too much money to make another career for himself in the theatre, and yet the offers from Hollywood had not improved in the wake of his critical success with *Lolita*. He had been out of England for too long to slip back easily into a studio life there, if indeed there was still such a thing at a time when films were becoming rather less Ealing and rather more European. Moreover, even if there had been regular work on his home territory, 'Queen Elizabeth is in her taxation system,' he memorably noted, 'very nearly as demanding as Pamela, and I certainly cannot afford to pay them both simultaneously.'

So it would have to be some kind of fresh exile, but this time in a European country where the taxation was reasonable and the transport rapid to whatever location might provide the next job. It took James no longer than Charles Chaplin or Noël Coward or David

135

Niven or William Holden or Deborah Kerr to realize the advantages of Switzerland.

First, however, there was the divorce to sort out. James went to a lawyer in San Francisco, on the reasonable assumption that any local Los Angeles man would almost certainly sell the story to one of the showbiz gossips, and eventually Pamela was persuaded to alter the charge from 'habitual adultery' to that of 'mental cruelty'. But the divorce took two years to complete, during which time James swore to his lawyer that he would never marry again – a promise he kept for almost ten years. In the meantime, 'totally cleaned out apart from the clothes he stood up in', according to Diana de Rosso, he returned to London and to a friendship with Kaye Webb, the children's writer who created Puffin Books, which had started during the war and her marriage to Ronald Searle.

'I think,' Kaye says now, 'that looking back I could probably have married James after his divorce, and in a way I rather wish I had, but we somehow neither of us quite plucked up the courage to go through all that again. We'd first met in 1942 when I was an assistant editor on a magazine called *Lilliput* and I found an article of his on the reject pile called 'Why I Beat My Wife' which was a jokey account of being a film star. I rather liked it so we ran it, and then he began writing other occasional articles for us. I was about to marry Ronnie Searle and James was always fascinated by artists, so the four of us became quite close friends and James was a marvellous godfather to our daughter. We never wanted him to go to America because I think we knew he was going to be unhappy there.

'It wasn't until the early 1960s that I saw him again very often, and by then he was terribly lonely and depressed because it had all gone so wrong. He used to just sit around in my flat looking hesitant. By then my marriage had gone wrong too, and I think we were able to be of some help to each other, but he was terribly withdrawn and hurt. In the years between Pamela and Clarissa, the 1960s in fact, there were occasional affairs with a Japanese actress and then the Italian Countess Crespi, but nothing terribly serious. When he came down to my flat in Brighton he was more often than not alone and constantly rueful about the way his life had gone so emotionally wrong. He was always rather secretive about his private life, but one had the sense of an increasing and finally unbearable loneliness, which is why I think he eventually married again: he just could not stay totally alone, even though people always thought of him as rather a loner. For quite a long while I think I was the best woman friend he ever had, and then he transferred that to my daughter Katie and he began to think of me as his god-daughter's mother and that was all. But I loved him very much and I think if I'd fought my way through all that reticence, as some other women did, then we might have ended up together. He had this terror of relationships going wrong, and that I think was all to do with Pamela and his time in California.'

James himself now began to grab at every offer which came along, simply as a way of settling his marital debts in Hollywood. The first of these was a little Italian disaster called *Finche Dura La Tempesta* briefly released in England and America as *Torpedo Bay*. 'Moderately gripping,' was the most even a trade paper could say about this wartime romance, 'and full of naive messages about international brotherhood.' Mason's next European co-production was fractionally more distinguished, if only because it put him somewhere near the top of a cast list which also featured Sophia Loren, Alec Guinness, Christopher Plummer, Mel Ferrer, Anthony Quayle, Omar Sharif and Stephen Boyd. *The Fall of the Roman Empire* was conceived by its producer Samuel Bronston and its director Anthony Mann as a successor to their equally epic and endless *El Cid*. Though it was made (thought Gerald Kaufman) with all the personal style of an IBM computer, there was something to be said for James as a Greek philosopher enduring torture by fire before meeting his end in a massacre which one of his own lengthy speeches has failed to quell.

There was also something to be said for regular and lucrative employment on a long location somewhere as far from Los Angeles as Madrid, where for the sake of art and alimony he could don his best bib and toga and think about his future. For Christopher Plummer, also on that location, 'the amazing thing was the way that he and Alec Guinness could take that truly appalling dialogue and make it sound acceptable. James knew an awful lot about how to steal movies through the back door, and give a performance that only really got noticed when the whole film was put together; so he would emerge with immense distinction having apparently been doing very little on the set. Away from the studio he was like a schoolboy suddenly set free from class: the divorce had given him his head, and he was able to do what he liked again. That romantic melancholy was always there but never any self-pity. He would describe his life and his career and his adventures as if they had all happened to someone totally outside himself. But by now he was starting to take films just for the money and the location, so of course he did end up in some quite awful things.'

And one or two very good things. His next offer in 1963 was back in England to join Anne Bancroft and Peter Finch in *The Pumpkin Eater*, Harold Pinter's screen treatment of a novel by Penelope Mortimer. Here Mason was cast as the jealous husband of an actress who has been having an affair with Finch, and he gave a performance of sardonic intensity which Dilys Powell, the film critic of the London *Sunday Times*, remembered as 'an extraordinary explosion of vicious fury'.

Mason himself was less then happy with Pinter's script, but his reservations were not widely shared and the general feeling was that it was a film which, unusually for its time, looked not only at women but with their eyes. By now James, too, was starting to look afresh at himself and his life. 'I brought a lot of bad publicity on myself over the years. When I settled in the United States, London papers attacked me as if I'd insulted England, and when I came back they could hardly wait to call me a failure. A lot of that was unfair and it did make me irascible, so one way and another I wasted a lot of time.'

By now the divorce had reached its final stages ('I don't hate my wife,' said James, 'but I certainly hate her lawyers') and there was, as the publicist Dick Guttman recalls, 'a wonderful moment in the court when Pamela appeared with a man who was rumoured to be a good friend of hers, and all the pressmen were lined up waiting for James to go over and punch him. Instead James just went over and tickled him under the chin and said "Naughty", and the cameramen went wild.'

Pamela got a settlement of a million and a half dollars, plus the Buster Keaton house and custody of the children, for whom James would continue to pay a thousand dollars a month in support until they came of age. It was, as one of the local papers noted, a total takeover by Pamela of everything that James had built up in twenty-three years of marriage and fifteen years of Hollywood: she told the judge at the last hearing about a 'grim and unhappy life' with her

138

husband: 'He would stay out all night and eventually he just left me.'

Mason as usual was less forthcoming, though he did reveal that he had given up his American residency and 'no longer had anything of value' in Hollywood. He also rashly announced that the one-million-plus settlement on his ex-wife was 'a mere fleabite'. 'If he gets many more bites like that,' retorted Pamela, who was still getting the last word, 'he will end up very moth-eaten indeed.'

And in truth James had so little money now that his first European home was a couple of rooms on the ground floor of a chalet near Vevey owned by his local Swiss bank manager: there, to the man-ager's amazement, 'this great film star could be seen sitting on a wooden packing case, with apparently no furniture at all'. Not surprisingly he rapidly began work on a television commercial for wine, and was still vaguely hoping to get back into productions of his own making. He and Peter Finch ('the two best screen actors of the English 1960s,' said Alan Bates, 'even when they work in rub-bish') had announced vague plans to form a joint company during the making of *Pumpkin Eater*, and James was still stubbornly muttering about the filming of *Jane Eyre*.

The reality, however, was to be on call as an actor to those who were able to get it together as film-makers, and the next of them was the writer–director Richard Brooks who, with the backing of Columbia, was about to make Conrad's *Lord Jim* with Peter O'Toole and saw Mason as ideal casting for Gentleman Brown, the Bible-thumping river pirate who gets spectacularly killed by a cannon filled with golden coins. O'Toole said afterwards that he wished he'd been given James's part instead of the title role, and Mason himself reckoned the best thing about the whole production was 'that we all got to visit the Far East in a style consistent with the demands of our respective agents'.

In the tradition of most Royal Command Performance films, this one did less than wonderfully with either critics or audiences but James had by now, in his mid-fifties, resigned himself to the life of a peripatetic character actor, taking the jobs as and when and where they occurred, and not worrying too much about the outcome. He no longer had a career to make, just a living, and that realization freed him to give some of the best performances of his entire career.

Not that his next was quite one of those: he and Robert Morley, my father, were somewhat implausibly cast as Chinese dignitaries in an epic of spectacular awfulness called *Genghis Khan*. 'If this is magnificence,' wrote Kenneth Tynan, 'give me the Ambersons. James Mason, equipped with an upper set of false rabbit teeth, brings off a genuine feat of impersonation as an effetely beaming Oriental diplomat.'

My father, cast as the Emperor, was not so sure: 'I don't think James was any less wildly miscast than I was, though it's true he did take a little more trouble with his pigtail. I just had mine glued onto my hat to save getting to make-up too early in the morning, but he wore his like a real wig. He was a curious man, usually on the phone to his agent asking about his next job, but very likable over lunch in a quiet sort of way.'

The next job was a strange Spanish-French co-production which hardly got a release in Britain and America despite a cast also featuring Melina Mercouri and Hardy Kruger. Called *Les Pianos Mechaniques* (*The Player Pianos*), it told of a middle-aged nightclub proprietor (Mercouri) and an alcoholic writer (Mason) in a Costa Brava holiday resort. James also now began turning up in one-shot British television dramas like *The Tormentors* and *A Tall Stalwart Lancer*, having apparently abandoned any attempt to form a coherent pattern to his career. The offer would simply come into his agent and, so long as the money looked solid and the part not too appalling, James would take it, providing in return what one critic called 'oases of good acting in deserts of dreary mediocrity'.

29

*'Instead of petering out, my career seems to be petering in as
I get older: I may no longer be the kind of star they can
raise money on, but for the first time in my life I'm making
films I really rather enjoy. Well, some of them anyway.'*

STILL URGENTLY SHORT of money to pay for the Swiss flat, its
much-needed furniture, the alimony and whatever retirement he
might eventually require, one which he often thought of financing
through his sketching rather than his acting, James was now aver-
aging three films a year to bring his total well up to eighty by the
end of the 1960s. The next three of these were, as it happened, all
hits, and in them he got back to increasingly important roles. For
The Blue Max, he was cast as an aristocratic Prussian during World
War I, a role in which, as his co-star George Peppard recalls, 'James
managed to manipulate the whole plot. He looked somehow much
older than he was, and I remember him telling me about being
stopped one night under a street lamp by a woman who said, "Excuse
me, but surely you are James Mason in a later life?" He seemed to
find that wonderfully typical of the way people thought of him.
Acting with him was like playing tennis with a really great player:
he made you better by being so good himself all the time, and by
making it look so effortless.'

Next came the film with Alan Bates and Lynn Redgrave that was
really central to James's return to English critical favour: *Georgy
Girl*. Written by Peter Nichols from a Margaret Forster novel, it
told of an ugly virginal duckling and the wealthy employer who

141

wants to make her his mistress, and James reckoned that not since *The Seventh Veil* twenty years earlier had he been involved in such a palpable commercial hit in his own country. For Lynn Redgrave, in her first major screen role, 'I couldn't have had a better start than with James. From the very first day on the set he treated me as an equal, never patronizing but always ready with advice and encouragement if you seemed to need it. They kept pulling the plug on the film because they said that James and I and Alan Bates didn't add up to much at the box office, but in the end we got it made because of James's enthusiasm for the quirkiness of the story, and the chance it gave him to go back to his Yorkshire accent. He took very little money for it, and we all thought it was just going to be a low-budget release, so when it became such a huge success it was all the more lovely for those of us who'd always had faith in it. James made me feel that if I tried I could do anything, even sing that song, and he told me always to close my eyes just before the camera started to roll. First because it would help to concentrate my mind on the scene, and second it would make my pupils look bigger and better. I've always remembered to do that.'

Mason got the second of his three Oscar nominations here, but now as a supporting actor, despite the fact that *Georgy Girl* had given him top billing over Alan Bates and Lynn Redgrave; and for the second time he was beaten, on this occasion by Walter Matthau for *The Fortune Cookie*. He did, however, get an immediate offer from Columbia and this time for a very strong spy picture which to some extent made up for the lost Oscar, and for another mistake James had made, in turning down the original James Bond script, *Casino Royale*, when it was being made for television in the mid-1950s.

This time the story was by John le Carré, and originally titled *Call From The Dead*. Paul Dehn made it over into *The Deadly Affair*, and the director was to be the man who had already worked with James on three New York television dramas (*The Hiding Place*, *John Brown's Raid* and *Silent Nights*) and was to go on with him over the next fifteen years to make *The Seagull*, *Child's Play* and *The Verdict*. This was his most faithful and constant director, Sydney Lumet:

'I always thought he was one of the best actors who ever lived. Whatever you gave him to do he would take it, assimilate it and then make it his own. The technique was rock solid, and I fell in love with him as an actor, so every time I came across a script I wanted to direct I would start to read it thinking is there anything here for James? He had no sense of stardom at all. He wanted good billing, and the best money he could get, but then all he ever thought about was how to play the part. In that sense he always reminded me more of an actor in a theatre repertory ensemble than a movie star, and it was what made him so good. He seemed to take unhappiness as part of his life's condition, rather than something he was supposed to do anything about, and yet even after we'd worked together so much I still sensed a privacy which one couldn't invade with James. He only really came to life when we discussed his work. Like Henry Fonda and Spencer Tracy he was always expected to be good on camera, so nobody ever bothered to notice just how good he was every time. There was a profound reliability about him as an actor, and that never changed. But I think he now had two classes of picture, the ones he despised and did for a lot of money and the ones he liked and did for very little.'

The Deadly Affair was one of those he liked, and his enthusiasm was reflected by the critics, many of whom wrote of 'Mason at his best' and 'a thriller to outrank Hitchcock'. As so often in his career, however, a couple of hits were followed by a straight run of more or less critically acceptable flops: between *The Deadly Affair* in 1966 and *Heaven Can Wait* back in Hollywood twelve years later, Mason made a grand total of thirty motion pictures, not one of which accounted for real money at the box office.

But that was no longer his problem. These were the years of his late fifties and sixties when he remained constantly employable at a supporting-actor level, never able to sell tickets alone above a title, perhaps, but guaranteed to bring a little respectability to the worst of Spanish-Italian co-productions, and considerable distinction to better efforts. Sometimes he took a film for the travel it offered, or to furnish his new flat above Vevey, or to buy a few paintings, or even a little jewellery for Yasuko Yama, a twenty-four-year-old Japanese actress whom he'd met on the *Lord Jim* locations and who was now increasingly to be seen at his side, though both were always quick and firm to deny any rumours of an engagement.

After *Georgy Girl* and *The Deadly Affair*, James stayed in England for *Stranger in the House*, which ended his run of luck on home territory; based on a George Simenon thriller, this was the story of a reclusive barrister who returns to his profession to solve a murder under his own roof. Raimu had already filmed it successfully in France as *Les Inconnus dans la Maison*, but surrounded by the youthful zeal of Geraldine Chaplin, Bobby Darin and Ian Ogilvy James merely looked as though he wished they were all involved in some quite different tale.

He then wandered off on his own to make *The London Nobody Knows*, a curious and haunting little documentary by Norman Cohen in which the camera followed James as he drifted around derelict East End music halls, public lavatories in Holborn and overnight dosshouses in an early example of the kind of fly-on-the-wall realism that would later win awards on television, but looked somehow out of place as a short subject on the wide screen.

Mason's lifelong interest in architecture, and his intelligence as an offbeat interviewer, would have well qualified him for one of those television series in which men like Alan Whicker or Peter Ustinov roamed the world finding out how and why other people in other countries lived in quite the way they did. In the absence of any such offers, he contented himself with appearances at film festivals in Cork, Acapulco and Toronto ('I go if they promise a prize and the air fare and a hotel, but sometimes just for the air fare and the hotel'), and increasingly reflective thoughts on his life, marriage and career:

'I seem to have spent a lot of my time being very angry, and in some ways I suppose I still am; that divorce cost me a whack and I go on paying quite a lot even now for the children, so I can't just settle back into old age and make one rather good film a year. I have to make money, which is why I can't just start out all over again as a director, which is what I'd really like to do. Looking back, I seem to have spent a lot of rather puny years doing what was offered to me. Hollywood has still not recovered from the death of Preston Sturges and they'll never make good comedies again out there, but there's still a chance for European film-makers because they avoid all the ludicrous grandeur and phoniness of California and just get on with the script in hand. Since I left there a few years ago I think I've acquired a lot more self-confidence in my work, but it would have to be one hell of a good script to get me back. People like Alec Guinness and Peter Sellers have managed to become international movie stars without ever having to live in Los Angeles for more than about a month, and I wish I'd been so lucky. The only questions

I ask myself now are do I like the script and have they got the money? If the answers are in the affirmative, I go ahead and shoot it.'

30

*'I seem to have become a sort of greasepaint gypsy, roaming
the known world in search of work on film locations. It's
not too bad a life, really; at least, I'm sure there are worse.'*

'Tosh, BUT NOT unmitigated', was James's own review of his next
film, a trendy comedy-thriller called *Duffy* in which he took third
billing to James Fox and James Coburn. His own private life now
acquired a certain comic intensity, as eagle-eyed airport reporters
noted him in constant company with the Chinese actress Yee-Wah
Young, who turned out to be the one they had thought of hitherto
as the Japanese actress Yasuko Yama. Miss Young, a versatile lady,
assumed different identities for different movies, but she was now
about to be firmly supplanted in James's affections by the Countess
Crespi, who lived near him in Vevey and was reported by neighbours
to be very keen on marriage to James. As usual he fought shy of any
such involvement. Asked once whether he wasn't afraid of dying a
lonely and isolated old man, he replied that he knew of no loneliness
quite so total as that of a married couple whose marriage had gone
sour. It was clear that he was speaking from considerable personal
experience.

James Coburn met Mason for the first time on *Duffy*: 'We were
to do three films together, but even by the end of the third I never
really knew him; the curious thing about playing a scene with James
was that you'd do your bit and then wait for his reaction, which
didn't seem to come at all. Not at least until next day, when you'd

see the rushes and realize that he had done it all, but so intimately that only the camera could pick it up. There was a magical thing that used to happen to his face on the screen: as he got older he got even more introspective, but he had always been the most wonderful film actor. You have only to look at *Julius Caesar*, where all the others are playing Shakespeare and he is playing Brutus. Unlike Niven or Granger he never really wanted to tell long anecdotes or hold people's attention at parties. He just used to watch them all the time, as if he was about to sketch them. Sometimes, of course, that's what he was doing.'

From *Duffy* James went into a heavily-costumed and bearded period piece, the Terence Young remake of *Mayerling* with Omar Sharif and Catherine Deneuve in the doomed-lover roles originally created by Charles Boyer and Danielle Darrieux. Mason was now cast as the Emperor Franz Joseph, and *Pandora*'s nostalgia freaks were delighted to find Ava Gardner in one of her last screen roles as his Empress. The film itself resembled an only occasionally animated costume parade, but James gave the relentless old father his personal brand of intelligent humanity, and his reward was to take home as usual the best of the reviews, such as they were.

It was by then the very end of the Sixties, and James was sixty years old: time perhaps for one last attempt at the role of something more than just a jobbing actor. The producer-director Michael Powell, for whom he had almost worked a quarter-century ago on *I Know Where I'm Going*, now came up with an idea for a film to be made largely on the Great Barrier Reef in Australia. Called *Age of Consent*, it was based on the Norman Lindsay novel about a world-famous Australian painter who goes home in search of his lost enthusiasm and vitality. Helen Mirren was to play the local girl he falls in love with, and one of the other attractions for James was the chance to co-produce with Powell, an off-screen responsibility that he took on here for the very last time and with traditionally mixed results.

Age of Consent was of crucial importance to James, in that it introduced him to his second wife, the Australian actress Clarissa Kaye who had a small part in the film and was to bring him in the last years of his life a peace and happiness that he had never known with Pamela. But as with all the productions on which he had been involved as anything else but an actor, the box-office results were extremely disappointing: 'A rambling, dawdling outback affair' was the general consensus, though the film did allow Jack MacGowran to give his last great performance as the drifter Nat Kelly, and it also gave an impressive screen start to Helen Mirren:

'I'd only been working for about a year, and this was the first film I'd ever done; James had seen me in a National Youth Theatre season and he and Powell decided I'd be right for the role, but once we got started Powell kept having vociferous fits of anger on the set, and James was just always there for me, very gently guiding and teaching as we went along. Having survived that brutal Hollywood world he was hugely experienced on the set, and tremendously generous to me. But after we finished the shooting he asked me to stay with him for a holiday in Switzerland, and I suddenly saw there how terribly lonely he was and how much he needed a woman like Clarissa to look after him. It was as though he'd never had anyone really by his side or on his side before. In the film he played another loner, a man on the run from any sort of social life, and that's really what he was, at least for as long as we were on the Barrier Reef. Back in Switzerland, he seemed altogether more sophisticated and worldly. I remember one night when he took me to the circus, Noël Coward and Charles Chaplin were also there. Because I was staying with James I met those two great legends at the end of their lives and I recall wondering what on earth they would be talking about, so I went over and Chaplin was saying, "It's my legs, Noël, my legs," and Noël was saying, "It's my back, Charlie, my back," and I suddenly realized how old they were all getting. Somehow you don't expect legends to age.'

And for James, at sixty *Age of Consent* marked the opening of a whole new life with Clarissa. She was then thirty-six and had been in the business since the age of two. 'My father was a panel-beater but with the most wonderful voice, and mother had always wanted to be a ballerina, so in a way they were both stage-struck. I was the middle one of three sisters, and from the time I was two they had me in dancing class. By the time I was five I'd played all the old peoples' homes and gaols and lunatic asylums in Sydney, singing Shirley Temple songs and tap-dancing, and from there I got into the circus as a contortionist, and then into musical comedies and revues. I also got married, very briefly, to an English pianist, but when that broke up people said I should take to more serious acting.

The best of his postwar romantic screen encounters: (*above*) with Ava Gardner in *Pandora and the Flying Dutchman* (1951), and (*below*) with Judy Garland in George Cukor's classic 1954 musical remake of *A Star is Born*

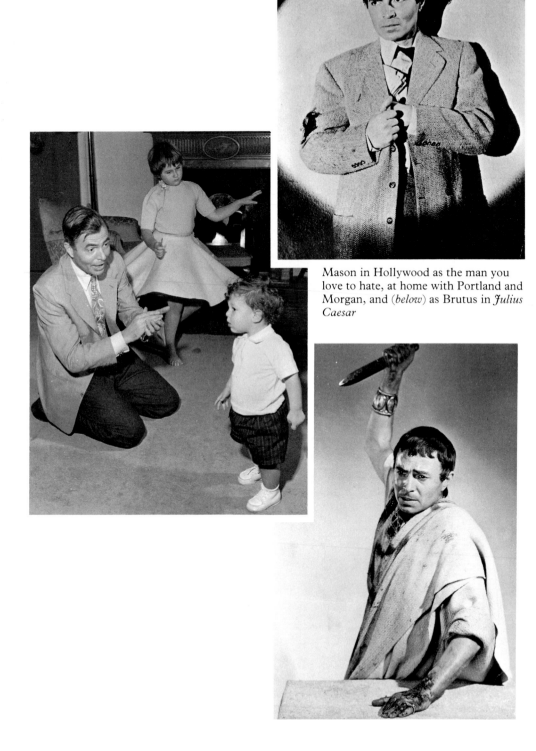

Mason in Hollywood as the man you love to hate, at home with Portland and Morgan, and (*below*) as Brutus in *Julius Caesar*

Three major movies: Rommel in *The Desert Fox* (1951), Aimsley in *Tiara Tahiti* (1962) and Humbert Humbert in Nabokov and Kubrick's *Lolita* (1962, with Sue Lyon)

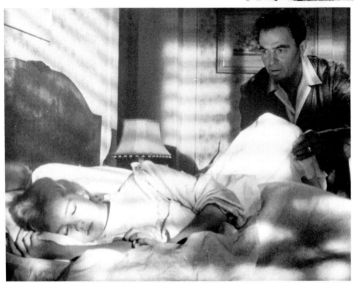

With Yasuko Yama cheerfully denying an engagement or a marriage in 1966, and with Sophia Loren on the set of *Decline and Fall of the Roman Empire* (1964)

In his Oscar-nominated performance in *Georgy Girl*

The children
growing up:
Portland with James,
and Morgan with
Pamela after the
divorce

With his second wife Clarissa Kaye and the director Jose Quintero rehearsing Brian Friel's *The Faith Healer* on Broadway in 1979

With his brother Colin and his parents at their diamond wedding anniversary

Survivors of *Julius Caesar*: Mason with Sir John Gielgud on location for *The Shooting Party* in 1983

James with some of his own drawings at the opening of an art exhibition at the Royal Institute, 1966. On the left is Simone Signoret; on the right is Sidney Lumet.

With Clarissa in London for the opening of *The Verdict* (1983)

'Screen Actor of the Century' (International Critics Award, Montreal World's Fair)

I began doing a lot of Tennessee Williams in club theatres around Sydney, and then I heard that there was this film of Michael Powell's coming up and that they wanted an actress to play one little scene in a bed with James Mason.

'So I auditioned and got it, despite the fact that they all said my eyes were too deep, and despite the fact that I was just getting over pneumonia. The woman in the film was supposed to be an old girlfriend of James's, and the whole scene was shot in bed, though when I arrived in my nightdress Powell looked appalled. I told him I was a thirty-six-year-old woman with a thirty-six-year-old body which sagged in parts and didn't look that good in the nude, but the real trouble was that because of the pneumonia I rattled every time I drew breath, and I think even James found that a little strange. I didn't like to explain how ill I'd been, in case I lost the job. Anyway I shot the scene with a temperature of about 103 and at the end of it we just got out of bed, said a polite goodbye and I thought that was the end of it. He was awfully sweet to everyone on that set, so I never thought he had taken any special notice of me until a few weeks later when someone else on that film said, 'You know he's very enamoured of you?' and I thought that was a lot of nonsense; but then a few weeks later I got this very long, sweet letter from him saying that I was a marvellous actress and how much he had enjoyed working with me and how he hoped I would get a lot more work because of our film. Then on the next Valentine's day I got a card from him, so then I did start thinking that maybe, just maybe, there was something special going on.'

As usual, though, it was not James who made the first move thereafter: like Clarissa he had determined never to marry again, and seemed now to have settled for the life of his own Flying Dutchman, roaming the earth to make movies with no real home anywhere. True, he had moved out of his bank manager's house in Vevey and into a modest little villa on the outskirts of the town where he was to die fourteen years later and where Clarissa still lives. There, between movies, he would go for long walks in the Swiss countryside, only occasionally accompanied by Portland or Morgan during school holidays, and apparently happy otherwise to sketch and start writing a book of overly discreet memoirs which was published to a somewhat muted press and public reception in 1981 as *Before I Forget*.

It irritated James that, unlike Niven, he could find no lucrative twilight career as an autobiographer, but given his extreme personal reticence and desperate desire to remain wherever possible the observer rather than the observed, it was not altogether surprising that readers and critics alike found the memoirs painfully shy, desperately short on anecdotage and lacking personal insights into himself or others. The book was, all too characteristically, the work of the invisible man.

Around Vevey he also kept himself very much to himself, finding little more in common with the English expatriate community there than he had ever found with the not entirely dissimilar one in the Hollywood hills. Mason was a loner, and might have gone to his grave as such had it not been for Clarissa. Like his first wife she was, and remains, a strong and dominant woman with a sharply etched identity of her own; unlike Pamela, she had achieved considerable success as an actress in her home country, and had now been making her own career for long enough to be willing to give it up for someone else's.

Financially she was unlikely to have had anything to gain from becoming the second Mrs James Mason, given the size of his alimony bills and the nadir to which his movie career had slumped soon after the time of their first meeting; professionally she had everything to lose, since James's Swiss tax status meant that he could spend very little time in either of the cities (London or New York) where Clarissa might have hoped to build on a promising Australian stage career. Moreover, time in either country would have to be 'saved' against the days when James would be required to film there, and that meant a life to be lived largely at his home in Switzerland or on endless foreign movie locations, essentially looking after a man who, in his early sixties, was almost twenty-five years her senior.

With all of that already obvious to her, the fact that Clarissa now pursued James halfway around the world armed with nothing more than a few encouraging letters from him and an air ticket paid for by a sudden, unexpected win on an Australian racetrack suggests that she must, from the outset, have loved him very much: a suggestion which her behaviour over the following years does nothing to deny.

From *Age of Consent* James went straight into two critically admired but commercially disappointing ventures, of which the first was again for Sidney Lumet. In a cast of immense distinction

(Vanessa Redgrave, Simone Signoret, David Warner, Harry Andrews, Denholm Elliott, Eileen Herlie), he was asked to play Trigorin for a film of *The Seagull*, his first and only return to Chekhov since his days with Guthrie at the Old Vic in the early 1930s. 'Extremely well acted,' thought *The Times*, 'but often painfully slow and cumbersome ... Mason's Trigorin, so diffident that when first introduced to Redgrave's Nina he can't even look her in the eye, is a fine study of a weak-willed, unworldly man who is only really happy when writing or fishing, but there has to be more to Trigorin than this surprisingly dull impression of a second-rate literary lion.'

At the National Theatre, however, Olivier was sufficiently impressed by Mason's return to the classics to offer him the role of Chebutikin in *Three Sisters* on film, the role that Olivier himself had played on stage there. Perhaps daunted by the footsteps in which he was being asked to follow, or else genuinely horrified by the lack of money involved, Mason turned down the offer and Olivier ended up again playing the part himself. It was not, in the event, much of a film, more a photograph of the original stage production at the Old Vic, but for all that it would have been good to see James just once, if only on screen, as a member of the National Theatre Company of Great Britain.

There was a sense, admittedly now growing fainter by the year and by the film, in which he still yearned for that sort of classical respectability: Lumet remembers the film of *The Seagull* as 'an absolutely unique experience, because we worked like a theatre company with a lot of rehearsal time on one location. It was an impossible film to finance, so we all did it on percentages with no salaries, and I remember on the plane flying back to London just holding hands with James almost in tears, aware that we'd come to the end of something very important in our working lives that we were probably never going to get the chance to recapture.'

31

'I'm a character actor: the public never knows what it's getting by way of a Mason performance from one film to the next. I therefore represent a thoroughly insecure investment.'

LATE IN 1969 James had made a rare return to his roots for the North Country filming of *Spring and Port Wine*, Bill Naughton's triumphant stage play about a tyrannical mill-working father reluctantly being forced to come to terms with a family he has bullied into incoherence. Redolent of *Hobson's Choice* and most of Priestley, this was a low-budget drama of relative values gone sour which would probably have looked better on television screens; but it was a useful reminder, as James now spent more and more of his working life on multinational co-productions, that he did in fact come from somewhere specific and was still just about capable of a convincing return there.

The film, however, did little at the box office, and James was once again left to hack his way around the world in an increasingly unrewarding search for a script that might do him a bit of good either artistically or commercially. Most actors in his perilous and fast-declining professional situation were inclined now to turn towards television or opening supermarkets; yet the curious thing about James was that, just as he was least happy in his most successful years as an actor, he now in a kind of gloomy screen twilight began to find himself perfectly content.

Of course he'd have liked more money and better pictures; but at long, long last, in a small house by a Swiss lake, with the prospect of Clarissa coming to see him occasionally and maybe even to marry him before long, he found a kind of happiness that had totally eluded him in California or before that back in England. Once he had finally paid off the divorce and given up any lingering dreams of being a producer or in some other way able to control his own career, once he finally settled for the peripatetic life of a strolling player, he found a kind of bleak humour in the worst of the work he had to do and a vague satisfaction when an occasional script came along to impress him.

Not that he was to hit any more of those until the mid-1970s; in the meantime he went to Hong Kong, partly so that he could again meet up with Clarissa who travelled there from Sydney, but ostensibly to take part in a curious fiasco called *The Yin and Yang of Mr Go*, a melodrama so awful that it sat on a studio shelf for about three years before finally being sold off in a heavily cut version to late-night American television.

'I arrived in Hong Kong,' recalls Clarissa, 'to find him making this really terrible film which thank God hardly anyone has ever seen. To my horror they gave me a very small part as some woman's lesbian lover. I remember asking James what on earth he had got me into, because I really didn't want to do it, but he said it was the only way he could think of to get me there so I did it just to be with him. Afterwards I said please just send me the air ticket and I'll come to wherever you are, but not playing lesbians in bad pictures, even for you. I don't think he'd bothered to notice quite how bad the part was for me.'

Around this time I once asked James how he viewed his life up to the present. 'As a rather poor three-act play,' he replied, 'The first act was the English theatre, which I really didn't care for all that much, the second act was the cinema, mainly in Hollywood, which I cared for even less, and the third act has been starting out all over again as a European character actor and that I find, rather to my own surprise, I like quite a lot. Mistakes? Yes of course, far too many; I should never have left England at the height of my fame there just after the war, least of all to have then to spend a whole year in America without being able to work at all; I should never have got myself into a divorce situation which wiped out all the money I ever made in Hollywood, because the only reason I was

153

ever there was to make money. I suppose you could say I've made a tremendous professional mess of my life, but oddly enough I can't really see it that way, and I don't live amid much regret. I just did what seemed right at the time and if it went wrong, well then I assumed that life was rather like that. It really doesn't do to hope or plan for too much; something usually happens to mess it all up. That's what happens with films too; you start with the best of intentions and often end up, as I did in *Lord Jim*, with a film that even my parents left at the interval before I'd made my entrance.'

While James and Clarissa were in Hong Kong on *The Yin and Yang of Mr Go*, they began to see a lot of the English journalist and war correspondent Ian Black. 'Towards the middle of the shooting the money began to run out,' he says, 'and James was always having terrible fights with the director, Burgess Meredith, because he demanded to be paid in dollars every week as I think he knew the kind of budget troubles they were in. Anyway I began to have dinner with James and Clarissa most nights, and it was then that he heard his mother had died back in Yorkshire. That threw him into a lot of reflection about his life. One sensed a tremendous, melancholy disappointment about the way Britain seemed to have declined to welcome him back with open arms. He felt that he'd not really been recognized by Hollywood either, and that because of his own inability to cope with the life and the people out there they'd denied him the Oscars that should really have been his on *A Star is Born*, *Georgy Girl* and *Lolita*. Some nights he seemed to take a kind of pride in his own isolation and independence, and other nights he seemed to wish desperately that he had managed to fit in with some sort of other life somewhere. He was still extremely bitter about how much the divorce had cost him, and I think somewhere in his soul he was always very troubled, though in the last few years there was a kind of settling down with Clarissa. He always needed a strong woman around him, and I think it gave him the security and the continuity he felt he didn't have in his career. It saddened him that actors like Bogarde and Burton seemed to get more attention and a better selection of roles, and he felt deep down that to have been an actor was still somehow not quite good enough, that he should really have stuck to being an architect which was rather more important in his scheme of things. He retained a tremendous disdain for the business of film-making; he really hated most producers, but if you

154

were any kind of a writer, he remained the most accessible of men. He was also always somehow unexpected: my favourite memory of this apparently very buttoned-up and conventional English gentleman is of him sitting in a Hong Kong hotel bedroom one night with Burgess Meredith, smoking a joint and reading quite wonderfully from James Joyce. He was a rare man.'

From Hong Kong and *Mr Go*, James went in quick succession through three more multinational catastrophes, of which the first (variously titled *Cold Sweat* and *L'Uomo dalle Due Ombre*) was, according to one critic, notable only for the sight of James wearing a funny hat, speaking with a Southern accent and dying gallantly. Charles Bronson and his wife Jill Ireland did most of the acting in an ungripping smuggling yarn, while James and Liv Ullmann did their best to look as if it wasn't really them.

Then came a sort of cold-spaghetti western, *Bad Man's River*, in which James played a Mexican revolutionary opposite Lee Van Cleef and Gina Lollobrigida and made the mental note that 'when shooting a western in Spain one should never tell oneself that it doesn't matter and no one will ever see it, because that is sure to be the one the Rank Organisation will choose to release in England'.

Last in this dire trio came a Spanish thriller called *Kill* (but later and more graphically retitled *Kill Kill Kill*) which managed to be a French/Spanish/German/Italian co-production but was shot in English, with a cast also led by Jean Seberg and Curt Jurgens. By now James's rage at the rubbish he was being offered was not improved by the realization that George C. Scott had succeeded where he had for so long failed, in setting up a film of *Jane Eyre* in which to play Mr Rochester, but he had at least made one major decision. If he was to roam the movie-making world making bad pictures for not terribly good money, he could at least do it with the woman he loved. Early in August 1971, in Switzerland and considerable secrecy, James and Clarissa Kaye were married, though there was no actual honeymoon as James was due in Munich the next morning to voice-over an American television documentary about the killing of Hitler. 'I know I look a lot gloomier than I really am,' he told a local reporter, 'but I'm really very glad to be married again after all. For quite a few months now, Clarissa has been known on foreign film locations as "Madame Mason" and having set up a domestic pattern which could quite easily be translated into a marriage, it seemed to both of us sensible that we should do so. I have become a rather fastidious old bachelor, crusty and hard to please, but Clarissa seems willing to deal with all that. We share the same interests, and are not trying to prove anything by marrying. I've learnt to survive by expecting failures. I have been through some very crabby times, and I got very bored of acting for a while, but it seems to be what I do best, so here I am still at it.'

As if to celebrate his domestic happiness, James now started a whole new career as a Bible-reader on Yorkshire Television's *Stars on Sunday*, reaching a large audience who had never seen him on the screen in anything but relatively minor work, but who now were won over by the most charismatic and distinctive voice since Gielgud (also, incidentally, a Bible-reader on that programme). The series was one of ITV's longest runners, and had the advantage of being shot in random sequence so that James could find a time when he wasn't busy on a film, spend three or four days in a Yorkshire studio armchair reading the Bible aloud, and then have the work cut up into weekly segments and shown every Sunday throughout an entire winter. 'Most English people in their middle years,' noted James, 'now sit stolidly in front of television sets and never go to a cinema. I liked reminding them I was alive.'

32

*'For years I was always regarded in American films as a
sinister foreigner: after* Lolita, *I became a sinister foreigner
who molested little girls. The truth is that I'm just a
character actor. I might have made better money if I'd ever
managed to become a superstar, but then again there are an
awful lot of unemployed superstars and I seem to be working
harder than ever.'*

THE TRUTH WAS of course, that James had lowered his sights. True,
there were still the occasional dreams of something better: early in
1971 Michael Powell was talking of filming *The Tempest*, which had
long been a dream of Gielgud's, and among the possible Prosperos,
after Sir John himself, the likeliest were reckoned to be James and
Rex Harrison in roughly that order. Sadly nothing came of the film,
which was also supposed to star Helen Mirren as Miranda, Mia
Farrow as Ariel and Peter O'Toole as Caliban, with a score by André
Previn and sets by Gerald Scarfe. With the collapse of that project
seemed to go Mason's last hopes of a return to the classics.

Instead he went back to Sidney Lumet for *Child's Play*, which
had the advantage of being made in a New York studio for Paramount
rather than on the Spanish locations that had recently been his low-
budget home. 'They say Spain and Italy are the new Hollywood,'
he noted dryly, 'and I suppose they are all just about as awful as
each other when it comes to making films, so one could spend one's
life drifting around in international co-productions. I just don't
much want to.'

On the way to America he did a nostalgic television documentary
about his Yorkshire birthplace (*Home, James*) but decided that he
was never really going to be at home anywhere except maybe in

Vevey with Clarissa. As with Pamela, he was trying to find work for his new wife in his films, partly to give her some reason for being on the set with him, but mainly because he strongly and guiltily felt that she had sacrificed an Australian theatrical career to marry him and should be given some chance to make it in Europe or America.

Child's Play was a reasonably faithful transposition to the wide screen of Robert Marasco's Broadway hit about sinister happenings at a Catholic boys' school, and it even had the same producer in David Merrick. Its showing in America was, however, in James's view 'more of a trickle than a release', though it allowed Pauline Kael to note the way in which he 'transforms an initially irritating bundle of neuroses quite miraculously into a figure of human dimensions. The way Mason inhabits a crumpled suit, his every grimace and shuffling step, bespeak the terrors of lonely old age and the painful self-denial of a cramped life.'

The film that came next was something altogether more enjoyable, at least in theory: for several years now, the great American musical writer Stephen Sondheim and his friend the actor Anthony Perkins had been fascinated by puzzles and mysteries and word and board games of all kinds. It was in Sondheim's Turtle Bay house that Anthony Shaffer first began to develop the idea of *Sleuth*, a thriller which was first offered to Mason for Broadway only to be unwisely declined before Anthony Quayle and then Laurence Olivier took it on: the working title was *Who's Afraid of Stephen Sondheim?*

But what came along now was *The Last of Sheila*, a movie thriller which Sondheim and Perkins cobbled together in the manner of a crossword puzzle rather than a film script: its plot was so thick with clues and cross-references as to be often almost impenetrable, while its final solution was actually contained within the lettering of the title itself. The central figure was an obsessively games-playing movie producer who invites a Hollywood group for a weekend on his yacht in the South of France: among them are Mason as an over-the-hill but once-great director, Raquel Welch as the star, Dyan Cannon as the sexy agent and Richard Benjamin as the frustrated writer. A murder has been committed (Sheila was the producer's wife), and the games are to discover the identity of the killer. Others die along the way, but an outline that had worked well enough for Agatha Christie's *Ten Little Niggers* (isolate a number of suspects and then work out the guilty parties) here got somehow caught up inextricably in its own elaboration. 'A crowning disaster,' thought the critic Rex Reed. 'The script requires a postgraduate degree in hieroglyphics to figure out, and the film is so full of impossible situations, demented logic and clues that are indecipherable even while they are being explained that the end result is one of total pretentiousness.'

But the filming was nothing if not eventful. An Arab Black September terrorist gang threatened to bomb the South of France location, Raquel Welch disappeared from the set to attend a movie premiere elsewhere, and James told the press that he had not enjoyed working with her. For Tony Perkins, the memory of James on that troubled location is of 'immense professionalism and a kind of quiet authority through all the chaos', while Richard Benjamin found 'a greatness about him in that he could do very ordinary conversation on the screen and make it real. The test of a movie star is whether, like Cary Grant and Bogart, they can talk on the screen and have nothing at all come between them and you in the audience. James was just like that: he was living for the moment, perfectly content to read the paper aloud to Clarissa on the set every morning if he found something he thought would interest her, and what was so lovely at that time was the way he seemed to be getting back towards his children again, making friends with Morgan and Portland as adults instead of the kids he had left behind in California. He seemed suddenly quite happy and relaxed, though he did find some of the women on the picture rather painful. "You know," he said to me on the yacht one night, "you and I should go off somewhere and make a really nice quiet picture about life in an all-male prison.".'

It was Molly Haskell for the *Village Voice* who noted that '*The Last of Sheila* is the perfect movie for New Yorkers, in that it shows that an all-expenses-paid vacation with a semi-hip group of movie people aboard a yacht in the Mediterranean can be as guarded and status-conscious and de-eroticized and full of stinging nettles as any Hollywood party ... it's a movie for people who feel superior to movie makers and movie audiences.'

There appear not to have been too many of those: *The Last of Sheila* did badly at the box office and has now become a collector-camp item for late-night television, though it deserves a slightly better fate. From it, Mason pressed on to *The Mackintosh Man* which again had a distinguished line-up (John Huston directing,

Paul Newman starring) and proved a major disappointment, this time because everyone in it seemed to be revisiting previous performances and James was redoing his suave villain from *North By Northwest* as the politician with the shady past. Huston himself admitted that they had never got the script right, or any kind of an ending until they were virtually shooting it, and a strong cast therefore finished up in considerable confusion.

James was perfectly content to drift from location to location, so long as he could spend a few weeks every year walking in or sketching the Swiss mountains. It also suited his inherent caution with money: from the moment he and Clarissa arrived on a film set they could charge their hotel bills and restaurant expenses to whatever the project was, and at a time when the scripts themselves certainly weren't giving him much satisfaction the idea that someone else was paying for everything never ceased to be a delight.

In these last ten years of his life, James averaged three major films or television movies every twelve months, and also found the time to do commentaries and commercial voice-overs as well as two final, though short-lived, stage plays in America. It was no kind of retirement, and it's hard to think of what James would have done in old age if he had not carried on with the acting.

His next film was *Frankenstein: The True Story*, a gothic horror mainly notable for Ralph Richardson as a blind yokel, John Gielgud as a fairly unlikely Chief Constable and James as the sinister doctor Polidori, giving what the *Daily Mirror* thought 'a performance of inscrutable villainy more suited to *The Mikado*'. The film was not much helped by the fact that it started out as a four-hour television mini-series and finished up at half that length in cinemas, thereby leading to certain confusions of plot. That alibi was not available for the next film to bring Gielgud and Mason together, *Eleven Harrowhouse*.

This was a diamond-heist caper with James as a faithful but under-pensioned company servant deciding to take one last profitable tilt at the system, and proof again that he was still leading a critically charmed life. As if aware that for years they had underrated him in good films, critics on both sides of the Atlantic now seemed determined to overrate him in bad ones, with the result that James was collecting some of the best notices of his life in work that was, at best, routine.

The Marseille Contract was another in that line, the makers of it apparently unsure how to spell the name of the city let alone how to make a good thriller there. James was the French Mafia boss whom Michael Caine was hired by Anthony Quinn to kill, and the result was at best a short-circuited *French Connection*.

This was followed by an adequate if uninspired and unnecessary remake of *Great Expectations*, in which James rashly took on the convict Magwitch and failed to live up to Finlay Currie's classically horrifying performance in the definitive David Lean version of thirty years earlier. Michael York, playing Pip this time around, nevertheless noticed 'a wonderfully quiet intensity about James, as though he was now, in his own rather private way, trying to break the mould of the recognizably elegant character player and take on roles like this convict, to surprise audiences and maybe also himself. He really was one of those protean actors who could tackle just about any part, and there are very few of those around any more.'

1974 was, even for James, an unusually crowded but otherwise fairly typical year. He took on six films: three Italian co-productions in all of which he played sinister heavies (*La Città Sconvolata, Gente di Rispetto* and *La Mano Sinistra Delle Legge*) in deeply unmemorable scripts; one average Anglo-American wartime thriller (*Inside Out* with Telly Savalas), one really terrible slave-trading melodrama (*Mandingo* with Susan George), and finally one film of merit but no real money, the Merchant/Ivory *Autobiography of a Princess*, in which James played the old tutor prompting the memories of Madhur Jaffrey.

Virtually a two-character film, rehearsed and shot in just over a week with the use of an extraordinary collection of home movies of 1930s' maharajahs only recently unearthed by the Merchant/Ivory team, this was a marvellously sustained evocation of a lost world and a requiem for a life, in which James gave one of the best performances of his last years.

Then it was back to the rubbish, specifically another Mafia chief in yet another Italian co-production (*Paura in Città*) and a Lew Grade *Voyage of the Damned* in which Orson Welles, Faye Dunaway, Oskar Werner, Max von Sydow and Malcolm McDowell all managed to look suitably embarrassed in what Russell Davies reckoned was 'one of the worst combinations of offensive trivialization and sheer dreariness since Stanley Kramer's *Ship of Fools* a decade earlier'. The director, Stuart Rosenberg, cast James and Orson as a couple of unlikely Cubans 'because James had the look of a man trying to keep a face on things while his heart was breaking: he had a lot of built-in torture behind the eyes. Away from the set, we used to have dinner occasionally, and you could sense that although privately he was very happy to have settled down with Clarissa, insofar as a travelling player ever settles down, professionally he was still disappointed by his character status and the way that the industry now seemed to be run by young people who knew nothing of his past. I even heard of one studio where they were still asking him to list his credits, at seventy.'

Undeterred by the awfulness of *Voyage of the Damned*, James went back to Lew Grade to give his Joseph of Arimathea in the epic Zeffirelli television film *Jesus of Nazareth*, and from there returned yet again to re-fight World War II as a German regimental commander, this time not Rommel but a reasonable facsimile thereof, in Sam Peckinpah's otherwise unmemorable *Cross of Iron*.

Late in 1976 he was home in his native Yorkshire ('after Harold Wilson, Huddersfield's most famous son,' announced the local paper) to play the evil chimney sweep Mr Grimes in *The Water Babies*, before taking on a role that Max von Sydow had been supposed to play in *The Passage* as a scientist on the run from the Nazis. 'It will be a flop,' James told his co-star Kay Lenz, 'you mark my words. All films that are made predominantly in thick snow are a flop at the box office. Somehow they make an audience feel uncomfortably cold and damp.'

As usual James was the best critic of his own movies: *The Passage* did indeed flop at box offices all over the world.

33

*'Status and salary are no longer so terribly important to me:
my desires and ambitions are just the same, though, as when
I started in this bloody business almost forty years and a
hundred films ago. I just want to do the best work I can
with the best people. The trouble is finding them.'*

AFTER SEVERAL YEARS in low-budget, multinational European
films, James returned to Hollywood early in 1977 for a run of three
pictures that he would once have characterized as Class A: Warren
Beatty's *Heaven Can Wait*, *The Boys From Brazil* and Sydney
Sheldon's *Bloodline*. The first of these was a remake of the 1941
classic, *Here Comes Mr Jordan*, with James cast in the old Claude
Rains role of the heavenly messenger who has to sort out the life or
death of the Beatty character after an accident. James's objection
here was only to the length of the shooting schedule. 'I got extremely
bored having to stay in California for four and a half months. It just
went on for too long. The picture is really quite a simple one,
and although I love Warren, his approach to making films is quite
different to mine. I do rather like to do things snappily.'

For Buck Henry, who co-wrote the new screenplay with Beatty
and also appeared in the film as Mason's celestial sidekick, 'James
was far and away the most touching actor of his time, and he managed
to move an audience without manipulating them. Ralph Richardson
was the only other actor I ever saw do that. But James still seemed
somehow unfulfilled as an actor and as a man, which was all part of
his emotional attractiveness: that Chekhovian melancholy was very
real to him, and there was always a kind of confusion because he

163

wanted at the same time an admiration that perhaps he wasn't fully getting, but also to be removed and distant from it all. He was a man of all kinds of confusions inside himself.'

The Boys From Brazil was a more gloomy project, a wide-screen treatment of Ira Levin's novel about the Nazi doctor (Gregory Peck) still performing ghastly medical experiments in the Amazon jungle. Laurence Olivier was the Viennese avenger on his trail, while Mason rather sheepishly played another of the jungle doctors. It turned out to be a ludicrous melodrama, which Philip French memorably subtitled *Send in the Clones*.

By now James was again getting restless for some respectable work: having made good money out of the last two Hollywood titles, he first went for a hat-trick by picking up the role that Olivier had rejected as one of the rival heirs slugging it out with Audrey Hepburn for a family inheritance in *Bloodline*. The location in Sicily was not a happy one, as the actress Beatrice Straight recalls: 'There was Irene Papas who kept saying she'd forgotten how to act, and James muttering he never again wanted to make a film he wasn't also producing and directing, and Audrey who'd come with her own bodyguard, but decided after a while, that on balance she'd rather be kidnapped by the Mafia than have to complete the picture; so all in all it wasn't one of the best, but James remained as ever a gentleman to the last, albeit a faintly disgruntled one.'

Then something better did happen along: the chance to play Dr Watson to Christopher Plummer in an above average Sherlock Holmes mystery called *Murder By Decree*. 'I am,' said James at the time, 'supremely suitable to play Watson because it's a role that for once is totally within my range. I could also have played Holmes, except for the unfortunate fact that I am physically quite the wrong shape. I don't see Watson as a buffoon: in the army he'd have been regarded as an intelligent man, and happily in this film he's been written as Holmes's equal. He was a good sort, an indomitable friend, able to make witty speeches at regimental dinners, dependable, full of common sense and dignity and integrity. He's the kind of man I would have liked very much. Holmes, on the other hand, was really rather weird.

'I'm not doing a lot of disguise at my age. I've never been like Olivier or Guinness who can work all those wonders with make-up. People always know it's me hiding behind the beard, and I don't really like to be doing a terrible lot of personality-changing any more. I'm really happiest now watching television with my sketch-book on my knee. I still think that perhaps I'd like to have been an artist or an architect rather than an actor. It really is such a silly profession, when you get right down to it. But thank heavens one doesn't have to do it all in California nowadays. The only things I really ever missed from there were my dentist and my doctor, and I've managed to make other arrangements in Vevey. I'm a man of habit. I do a bit of reading, a bit of painting, a bit of gardening, a bit of housekeeping and shopping, and a bit of strolling around the mountains. My wife sees to it that I get all the vitamins I need, and I do half an hour of exercise in the morning, though thank heavens we don't have a swimming pool. The smell of all that chlorine reminds me of ghastly associations with southern California. I think perhaps I got there at the wrong time: I would have liked to have been the Warren Beatty of my day, a producer of flair and a warrior-merchandizer as well as a brilliant actor. Somehow I never quite managed all of that.'

For David Hemmings, cast as the police inspector in *Murder by Decree* amid an extremely strong company which also included John Gielgud, Anthony Quayle and Frank Finlay – causing the critic Derek Malcolm to note that if the author was turning in his grave it would only be to watch them – the most important thing about Mason was 'the wit behind the eyes and that tantalizing, suggested wickedness in the voice. He never locked himself into any one characterization or role the way that many actors of his generation did, and therefore he remained totally professional but totally unex-pected, and that was very exciting to work with. True, he and Plummer never quite achieved that definitive relationship of Basil Rathbone and Nigel Bruce in all those earlier Holmes films, but theirs was perhaps a more interesting relationship forty years later. I think to some extent James had his career slashed by the demands of world cinema, so that he never had the continuity of an English career which might perhaps have done him more good in the long run, but by the time I got to know him he was just about to have his seventieth birthday and really past caring about all of that.'

Mason was keen to stay working. From *Murder By Decree* he went back into television, first to narrate a major Thames series on the history of Hollywood (a somewhat ironical assignment for one who still so cordially loathed the place), and then to appear in a gothic horror by Stephen King called *Salem's Lot*. He turned down a Michael Winner assignment on *Firepower*, firstly because it involved a cockfight which he decided was morally unacceptable on screen, and secondly because he had now, in his seventy-first year, decided the time was right for one last assault on Broadway.

Returning to the New York stage for the first time since the disastrous *Bathsheba* thirty-two years earlier was not a decision to be taken lightly; for the first time in his life Mason had now achieved a kind of contentment with Clarissa, ambling from location to location and, when rarely not in work, pottering about the Swiss lakeside where (like Eric Ambler and Nabokov) he lived a life of almost total seclusion. 'People are always asking,' he said to me irritably once over lunch at about this time, 'what on earth Clarissa and I find to do all day in Switzerland, when the whole point is that we don't actually do anything.'

But there were two powerful reasons why he wanted to face the Broadway battleground again: it remained almost the only one he had never conquered, and he was desperate to give Clarissa a chance of stardom. Typically, he chose to do all of that in the most difficult way imaginable. Rather than selecting some easy drawing-room comedy, or a minor but well-tested classical vehicle in which he would be as safe as (for instance) Rex Harrison has been on stages around the world this last decade, James chose an extremely difficult and demanding new play by Brian Friel which consisted of three characters delivering four very long monologues but never actually meeting on stage.

There is no doubt, at least in my mind, that Friel is the most important Irish dramatist of his generation and that *Faith Healer* is a major play. But on Broadway, which had already given up any claim to be a serious home for new drama, with an actress who had never worked on an American stage and Mason's own long absence from the theatre all to be taken into consideration, the project fell somewhere midway between courageous and foolhardy. For the producer Morton Gottlieb, who had tried to tempt Mason back to Broadway a few years earlier with what was a vastly more successful American premier, *Sleuth*, this was the realization of a long-held ambition.

'I'd always wanted to see him back on the New York stage, but

Sleuth came fairly soon after his divorce and he said that because of what it had cost him he couldn't possibly afford to do anything but movies. Now, however, times had changed, and he was keen to work with Clarissa who obviously made him very happy. We all knew we had a very highbrow play which would need a lot of help from the critics, and to keep costs down we were really only paying him expenses: but he was in marvellous shape and great form, terribly happy to be working with Clarissa and I never saw him depressed, even after the reviews were in. Even on a tricky, difficult and special play like that one, there was never anything negative about him. He gave you a constant sense of the positive.'

Rehearsals were not easy, as Clarissa recalls:

'James was really keen for me to get back to work as an actress. He used to say that he wanted it to be like it was in *A Star is Born,* not with him walking into the sea or anything like that, but just with my career gently overtaking his. So he was always on the look-out for a joint project and he'd had one or two offers from the Royal Court, which he couldn't take up because of his English tax situation, so when this one came along he was just thrilled. But early in rehearsals the director Jose Quintero wanted to get rid of me, and they did in fact replace the other actor in the show before we got to Broadway where Donal Donnelly played it. But James said he wouldn't work without me, so we took it up to Boston and then on to Broadway. It was not much of a success.'

Even in London, *Faith Healer* met with indifferent reviews, and it wasn't until an Abbey Theatre production in Dublin a year or two later that the play began to come into its own. The story is of a travelling spiritualist with apparently magical healing properties, his wife and his manager, all of whom narrate to the audience an account of their life together on the road, apparently curing the blind and the crippled and the mad but seldom fixing their unyielding despair.

It is a dark and powerful play, and the lasting memory for those of us lucky enough to have seen it in the fortnight that *Faith Healer* survived on Broadway is of James standing on a bare stage in a half-empty theatre, dressed in a rumpled overcoat and giving, in ghostly monologue, the most powerful performance of his career. As Jack Kroll noted for *Newsweek*: 'Mason is now a beautiful old man, and perfect for this part. His face glows with a yearning and bemused innocence, a galvanic humility, a hope and a despair that seem to have collided within him and whose collision has become an embrace.'

Even that, however, was not enough for a Broadway audience who were in no mood for the dark intensity of Friel's visions, and the play stayed true to James's New York track record. A few months later he and Clarissa tried out one other new play by Leslie Stevens, called *Partridge in a Pear Tree*, but that too closed very quickly, in Washington, and with it went the last remnants of James's career as a stage actor.

34

*'I have simmered down to the conclusion that although
society needs a certain amount of work from architects and
builders, it really does not need very much from actors, so I
have stopped doing too much in my old age, though I retain
this juvenile optimism that something fascinating will be
around the corner or behind the next tree. Even if it's only
death.'*

JAMES NOW HAD four more years to live and eight more films to
make, two of which were to be among the most distinguished of his
entire career. Neither of those, however, was *North Seas Hijack* in
which he played an Admiral of the Fleet trying to regain a British
oil rig from hijackers. The film was originally called *ffolkes* until a
Fleet Street cartoonist of that name objected to the similarity, and
it also starred Roger Moore and Anthony Perkins under the direction
of Andrew McLaglen.

'James by now was getting on a bit,' McLaglen says, 'but he arrived
on the set every morning word-perfect and his was still a very
powerful name to have on a film. He reminded me faintly of Richard
Burton in that they both reached a point in their lives when they
were really happier on a film set than anywhere else, even if the film
was not going to be all that special. He just seemed to like the life
and the crew and the other players, and although he still kept himself
to himself until he really knew who you were, he was always very
wary and chary of people, he made a location seem like some gentlemen's club with himself as one of the quieter members, but
somehow always there and infinitely reliable.'

Critics were now in little doubt that Mason had, characteristically
unobtrusively, become one of the great screen stars of the century.

It was Vincent Canby for the New York *Times* who wrote of his ability 'to give unexpected dimension by creating characters that command attention . . . for some time I've been thinking that Mason was becoming a better and more interesting actor with the passage of time, but having recently reseen *Lolita* and *North by Northwest* and *Georgy Girl* it now occurs to me that he has always been superb. He is in fact one of the few film actors worth taking the trouble to see even when the film that encases him is so much cement.'

By now, and not for the first time, James's first wife and at least one child were making bigger headlines than he was: as he retreated into a still quieter lakeside life in Vevey with Clarissa, Pamela got embroiled in a massive battle to retain family shares in a Yorkshire textile business and Morgan took a high-profile White House job as an aide to the Reagans. But James stayed well away from all of that, content merely to carry on filming and utter the occasional architectural broadside at what he saw as the desecration of Hyde Park, first by the army barracks and then by the Hilton that had been built on its borders.

Professionally he took a bit part in a less than wonderful television remake of *Ivanhoe*, playing a Jewish moneylender, and then went on to the rather starrier *Evil Under the Sun*, one of the Ustinov-as-Poirot Agatha Christie thrillers, which brought him together with Roddy McDowall:

'When you meet an actor you've admired all your life, and then have the bonus of becoming a friend for his last few years, you desperately want not to disappoint, and so I spent a lot of that film making sure I got everything right. He had a wonderful sense of humour, not always appreciated, and based on a sort of wry awareness of his own shortcomings. He was the most timeless and penetrating of actors, deeply underrated, and there was an intelligence about him alongside that margin of glamour and mystery.

'Clarissa was just wonderful with him, very protective but also feisty and very funny, and giving him what were undoubtedly the best years of his life. On screen he was a truth machine, always bringing an investment to the film by illuminating his role with things that nobody else had ever seen in it. On the set he would give it all he'd got, and then just go and sit very quietly next to Clarissa doing the crossword and she would do the needlework and they'd read bits out of the paper to each other. There was something marvellously old-fashioned and touching about their relationship. There have been certain people in my life like James (and Gladys Cooper and Noël Coward and George Cukor) whom I miss more than all the others, because selfishly I always felt better when I was around them. And yet somehow one could never tell James how much he meant to other people: that reserve was there to the very last.'

By now James had, at long long last, come to a moment in his life when he could pick and choose the work: he therefore abruptly declined to appear as the Duke of Edinburgh in a tasteless tele-drama about the wedding of Charles and Diana, but did somewhat mysteriously agree to be caught dancing with several Radio City Rockettes and Robert de Niro in an American television special where it was briefly possible to glimpse him looking, just for once, as if he was having a good time at a party. But now it was increasingly Clarissa who took charge of his career:

'We were a couple of gypsies, living from film to film, but James was always worried about money and where the next job would be coming from, and he had some very major disappointments even towards the end of his career. Sidney Lumet always said that after all their films together James was his favourite actor, but then along came *Network* and he gave it to Peter Finch, so James was very uneasy when he heard that there might be a job in Lumet's next picture, which was *The Verdict*. The part he was first offered was the one eventually played by Jack Warden, and Lumet was doubtful that James would do it, but I knew he badly wanted to get back into a Class A film so I made him ring Lumet. Then what happened was that Burt Lancaster dropped out, so James got the better role of the lawyer. But I don't think he would have gone back to Lumet if I hadn't made him pick up the phone. His pride was very hurt over *Network*, and understandably. Yet he was still a working actor, and he knew he had to take it.'

The performance that won James his last Oscar nomination was the first of two which, given in the very closing months of his life, came as conclusive proof of his pre-eminence as a screen actor. The part of Concannon, the hugely powerful law-firm boss who goes into courtroom battle against Paul Newman, is, in David Mamet's *Verdict* screenplay, one of the major roles given to an actor in the 1980s. As Jack Warden says of his first appearance 'it's the Prince of fucking

Darkness', and James spent the entire picture at his most mesmerically Satanic.

Even so, he lost out on the Oscar to Lou Gossett for *An Officer and a Gentleman,* and went back to guesting in television mini-series (*AD, George Washington*) before making a fleeting appearance in *Yellowbeard,* a deeply unfunny pirate romp not greatly helped when its star Marty Feldman died during the shooting.

But Mason himself was no longer in the best of health. As he approached his seventy-fourth birthday, doctors in Vevey diagnosed a heart condition and recommended that he wear a pacemaker, one which was already in place when he made a film called *Alexandre* for Swiss television. He then turned up briefly in a minor Cannon thriller called *The Assisi Underground* which was mercifully never widely released, despite a cast also featuring Max von Sydow and Ben Cross.

Following that came the offer of something more impressive: a BBC television film of Graham Greene's novella *Dr Fischer of Geneva* with Alan Bates. Immediately before shooting started he went back to America for what was to prove the last time, not now to make a new film but to help publicize an old one. Ronald Haver of the Academy of Motion Picture Arts and Sciences had spent several years unearthing and restoring the footage of *A Star is Born* that had been cut at the time of its first release, and James now appeared on stage at Radio City to introduce the fully reconstructed version and recall his joy at working with Garland and Cukor.

Returning to start work on *Dr Fischer,* he received the news that Paul Scofield had been badly injured in a carriage accident on the first day of filming *The Shooting Party,* an account of an aristocratic Edwardian prewar society on the verge of being as surely blasted away as the birds they shoot during a country-house party. James and Clarissa immediately realized that the part of Sir Randolph Nettleby, host of the gathering, was one that Mason could hardly refuse to take over from the injured Scofield; on the other hand, he was already in the middle of filming for the BBC. The strain of starring in two films being shot simultaneously in different countries (*Dr Fischer* was on a Swiss location) would clearly be considerable, especially on a man of seventy-four with a pacemaker. On the other hand, only Clarissa really knew how ill he was and yet how desperately he wanted to make those last two pictures, ones which

172

would allow him (with *The Verdict*) to end his career on a hat-trick of distinguished performances in major works, not a luxury he had often been allowed to enjoy in a career of more than a hundred movies.

'For the last three years of our life together,' recalls Clarissa, 'I was constantly terrified about his health because there were some nights when he scarcely seemed to be breathing at all, and I used to reach out in bed to hold him and make sure he was still alive. There was a cemetery scene in *Dr Fischer* that I found horrifying, because I was sure I was going to lose him to one before too long, and I simply couldn't imagine having a life alone again. I used to have terrible nightmares about being left in the world without him, but he was never going to be the sort of husband you could push around in a wheelchair. He wanted to go on working as hard as he could for as long as he could, and that was exactly what he did.'

35

*'How do I wish to be remembered, if at all? I think perhaps
just as a fairly desirable sort of character actor.'*

TOWARDS THE END of James's life, one of his near neighbours and
rare friends in Switzerland was the English screenwriter and novelist
Bill Fairchild: 'We'd first met in his very early Swiss days, when he
was just getting over the Pamela marriage and trying to stay single
despite the pressure of some rather strong ladies like the Countess
Crespi. But then Clarissa came along and he seemed to settle down
very happily with her, living in that very quiet community of Eric
Ambler and Brian Aherne who hardly ever seemed to go out or get
photographed or lead public lives at all. James was the most un-
actory actor I ever knew: we only ever did one film together, that
terrible *Mackintosh Man* which Huston asked me to rewrite halfway
through the shooting, staying one day ahead of the camera. John
said we needed a new location so I asked James if there was anywhere
he fancied going and to my amazement he said Malta, so we set some
of the film there.

'On that location he as usual kept himself very much apart, kept
talking about what a good actress Clarissa was and how she ought
to be getting much more work; in some senses he was a very weak
man in need of strong ladies, but he also rather wanted them to
succeed in their own right, a sort of Olivier/Vivien Leigh thing in
miniature. There's no doubt that Clarissa changed his life, taught

him how to be healthy, gave him a real desire to go on working and living, although I do think at the end he pushed himself too hard, doing those two last films back-to-back.

'There's no doubt that towards the end he was looking very grey, but he didn't want anyone to know about the pacemaker because like all actors he was terrified of not getting any more work if people started to think he might be uninsurable. One got very fond of him, without ever really feeling one had ever managed to know him very well.'

The Shooting Party brought James together with Gielgud for the last time, but, with John playing the relatively minor role of the conservationist, there was no doubt that on this occasion it was James's film, and as Pauline Kael observed for the *New Yorker*, 'He goes out in glorious style, using a mild, ageing man's voice and his querulous, cracked inflections make us smile ... his face, and especially that plangent voice, are so deeply familiar that when we see him in a role that does him justice, there's something like an outpouring of love from the audience to the screen. Mason validates our feelings: he uses his own physical deterioration for the role, yet he never turns into a grand old man or indulges in a quaver that isn't a funny, integral part of the country squire who's conscious that he's losing his grip ... when they play their one scene together Mason and Gielgud are like soft-shoe artists; they bring suavity to their teamwork, with Mason matching his melancholy warble to Gielgud's melodious whines; they're even more hilarious than Gielgud and Richardson once were ... and when, towards the close of the film, Mason has a scene overladen with the possibilities of pathos and grandeur, he pulls back; he underplays magically. No one could accuse James Mason of not acting like a gentleman.'

For Edward Fox, working with Mason on that film, 'There was this courteous, well-mannered, non-complaining, exemplary actor in total command and control, but looking suddenly terribly ill and grey. He never flagged or faltered, never missed a day's shooting, but he was being extremely economic with what strength he had and I think he must have known he was close to the end, but determined to go out with one more really classic performance. Which of course he did.'

But then it really was all over. Back in Switzerland, in July 1984, Clarissa remembers 'he did seem very tired, and of course ever since

175

the pacemaker I'd been worried about him, but then one night we were supposed to go out to dinner and he suddenly said he felt terrible so we went to bed, and then in the night he had this appalling pain right through his back so I rushed him to the hospital and it was all horribly quick, which perhaps was for the best as he was a man of the moment. I don't think he or I would have wanted him to have a living death in a wheelchair. He never wanted to get old. Even in his coffin he looked about fifty, and back at the house there were still three scripts piled up waiting for him to agree to make them.'

James Mason died in a Lausanne hospital on 27 July 1984 at the age of seventy-five; the London *Times* next morning wrote of 'a highly intelligent and creative cinema performer', while the *Los Angeles Times* noted 'a wracked nobility in the most gentle and subtle of actors'. Characteristically, perhaps, Pamela's memories were somewhat more mixed: 'He was very embittered that his career in Hollywood didn't work out better, and in his fifties his personality changed drastically; he suddenly wanted to drive fast cars and go out at night with ladies. He said his whole life had been for nothing, and that he wasn't satisfied with anything that he had or anything he had done ... I often wonder how well I really knew him, or how well he knew himself. You must, in the end, do what you can to be happy; the tragedy is that he didn't do that all his life.'

And even after James's death, the controversy that had for so long been a part of his marriage to Pamela continued, as Clarissa was locked into a long and bitter (and in early 1989 still continuing) court battle with Portland and Morgan over the provisions of Mason's will and his inheritance.

One or two of the obituaries wrote inevitably of 'the nearly man', the actor who had never quite scaled the heights of the classical theatre where he started, nor yet of the Hollywood cinema to which he emigrated; but the general feeling among press and public alike was of regret that so powerful a screen actor had only at the very end of his long career begun to get the kind of sustained critical and public recognition that had for so long been his due, and regret also that he had gone un-Oscared and unknighted to his grave, though conscientious objection and tax exile had a bit to do with the latter omission.

A memorial service for James Mason was held at St Paul's, the actors' church in Covent Garden; but it was at a simple lakeside funeral in Vevey that his friend Bill Fairchild delivered the best and simplest epitaph: 'In a noisy world he spoke quietly, and yet his voice will be remembered by millions who never knew him.'

Appendix

Stage

1929   *The Bacchae* by Euripides (New Theatre, Cambridge)

1930   *The Fairy Queen* by Henry Purcell (New Theatre, Cambridge)

1931   *The White Devil* by John Webster (ADC Theatre, Cambridge)
         The Rascal by Vanko Kevnov (Theatre Royal, Aldershot)

1932   *Old Heidelberg* by William Mayer-Foster (Bournemouth Pavilion)
         The Torchbearers by George Kelly (Bournemouth Pavilion)
         Private Lives by Noël Coward (Torquay Pavilion)
         John Ferguson by St John Ervine (Torquay Pavilion)
         The Fanatics by Miles Malleson (Devonshire Park Theatre, Eastbourne)
         On tour with the Brandon Thomas Company:
            At Mrs Beam's by C. K. Munro
            The Great Adventure by Arnold Bennett
            Home Chat by Noël Coward
            Nothing But The Truth by James Montgomery
            The Queen Was In The Parlour by Noël Coward
            The Skin Game by John Galsworthy
            The Vortex by Noël Coward

1933   *The Prisoner of Zenda* by Edward Rose (Hull Repertory Theatre)
         Hay Fever by Noël Coward (Hull Repertory Theatre)
         Lean Harvest by Ronald Jeans (Hull Repertory Theatre)

The Lady From Albaquerque by Serafin and Quinero (Hull Repertory Theatre)

In The Zone by Eugene O'Neill (Hull Repertory Theatre)

Escape by John Galsworthy (Hull Repertory Theatre)

The Importance of Being Earnest by Oscar Wilde (Hull Repertory Theatre)

The Fake by Frederick Lonsdale (Hull Repertory Theatre)

Secrets by Besier and Edington (Hull Repertory Theatre)

Tusitala by Hines and King (Hull Repertory Theatre)

Hay Fever by Noël Coward (Croydon Repertory Theatre)

Gallows Glorious by Ronald Gow (Croydon Repertory Theatre and Shaftesbury Theatre)

After All by John van Druten (Croydon Repertory Theatre)

Twelfth Night by William Shakespeare (Old Vic)

The Cherry Orchard by Anton Chekhov (Old Vic)

Henry VIII by William Shakespeare (Old Vic)

Measure for Measure by William Shakespeare (Old Vic)

1934   *The Tempest* by William Shakespeare (Sadler's Wells)

The Importance of Being Earnest by Oscar Wilde (Old Vic)

Love For Love by William Congreve (Sadler's Wells)

Macbeth by William Shakespeare (Old Vic)

Queen of Scots by Gordon Daviot (New Theatre)

Julius Caesar by William Shakespeare (Dublin Gate Theatre)

The Provok'd Wife by Sir John Vanbrugh (Dublin Gate Theatre)

The Drunkard by William Smith (Dublin Gate Theatre)

1935   *Magic* by G. K. Chesterton (Dublin Gate Theatre)

Wuthering Heights (Dublin Gate Theatre)

Lady Precious Stream by S. I. Hsiung (Dublin Gate Theatre)

Othello by William Shakespeare (Dublin Gate Theatre)

The Abbé Prévost by Helen Waddell (Croydon Repertory Theatre)

1936   *Luck of the Devil* by Ladislav Fodor (Arts Theatre Club)

Parnell by Elsie Schauffler (Dublin Gate Theatre)

Flying Blind by James Mason and Pamela Kellino (Arts Theatre Club)

179

1937   *Pride and Prejudice* by Christine Longford (Dublin Gate
       Theatre)
       The Road to Rome by Robert Sherwood (Embassy and Savoy
       Theatres)
       Miserable Sinners by Nigel Balchin (Ambassadors Theatre)
       A Man Who Was Nothing by Flannery and Browne (Q
       Theatre)
       Bonnet Over the Windmill by Dodie Smith (New Theatre)

1938   *The Heart Was Not Burned* by James Laver (Dublin Gate
       Theatre)

1939   *Sixth Floor* by Alfred Gehri (St James's Theatre)
       On tour for ENSA:
           Eight Bells by Percy Mandley
           I Killed the Count by Alec Coppel
           Heroes Don't Care by Margot Nevill

1940   *Jupiter Laughs* by A. J. Cronin (King's Theatre, Glasgow)
       Divorce for Christobel by George and Margaret Matthew
       (Grand Theatre, Blackpool)

1941   *Jupiter Laughs* by A. J. Cronin (New Theatre)

1943/4 On tour for ENSA:
           Jeannie by Aimee Stuart
           Gaslight by Patrick Hamilton
           Petticoat Fever by Mack Reed

1945   On tour for the American Red Cross:
           Othello by William Shakespeare
           Made in Heaven by Hagar Wilde
           The Road to Rome by Robert Sherwood

1947   *Bathsheba* by Jacques Deval (Ethel Barrymore Theatre, New
       York)

1954   *Measure For Measure* by William Shakespeare (Stratford,
       Ontario)
       Oedipus Rex by Sophocles, translated by W. B. Yeats (Strat-
       ford, Ontario)

1957   *Paul and Constantine* by Dario Bellini (La Jolla Playhouse, California)

1958   *Midsummer* by Vina Delmar (Ivorytown Playhouse, Connecticut)

1979   *Faith Healer* by Brian Friel (Longacre, New York)

1980   *Partridge in a Pear Tree* by Leslie Stevens (Washington)

Film

Years given here are the dates of first British release.
Years and sequences given in the text are those in which the films were made.

1935   *Late Extra* (Fox British) with Virginia Cherrill, Alistair Sim, Ian Colin; dir: Albert Parker.

1936   *Twice Branded* (GS Enterprises) with Robert Rendel, Lucille Lisle, Ethel Griffies; dir: Maclean Rogers.
Troubled Waters (Fox British) with Virginia Cherrill, Alistair Sim, Raymond Lovell; dir: Albert Parker.
Prison Breaker (Columbia Grand) with Andrews Engelman, Ian Fleming, Marguerite Allan, Wally Patch; dir: Adrian Brunel.
Blind Man's Bluff (Fox British) with Basil Sydney, Enid Stamp-Taylor, Barbara Greene, Iris Ashley; dir: Albert Parker.
The Secret of Stamboul (Wainwright/GFD) with Valerie Hobson, Frank Vosper, Kay Walsh, Laura Cowie; dir: Andrew Marton.

1937   *The Mill on the Floss* (National Provincial) with Frank Lawton, Fay Compton, Geraldine FitzGerald, Griffith Jones, Athene Seyler; dir: Tim Whelan.
Fire Over England (Korda) with Laurence Olivier, Flora Robson, Vivien Leigh, Leslie Banks, Robert Newton, Raymond Massey; dir: William K. Howard.
The High Command (Fanfare) with Lionel Atwill, Lucie Mannheim; dir: Thorold Dickinson.

181

Catch as Catch Can (Fox British) with Finlay Currie, Margaret Rutherford; dir: Roy Kellino.
The Return of the Scarlet Pimpernel (London Films) with Barry K. Barnes, Sophie Stewart. Margaretta Scott, Henry Oscar; dir: Hans Schwartz.

1939   *I Met A Murderer* (Grand National) with Pamela Kellino, Sylvia Coleridge, William Devlin; dir: Roy Kellino.

1941   *This Man Is Dangerous* (Rialto/Pathé) with Mary Clare, Margaret Vyner, Frederick Valk; dir: Lawrence Huntington.
Hatter's Castle (Paramount British) with Robert Newton, Deborah Kerr, Emlyn Williams, Henry Oscar; dir: Lance Comfort.

1942   *The Night Has Eyes* (US: *Terror House*) (Associated British/Pathé) with Mary Clare, Wilfred Lawson, John Fernald; dir: Leslie Arliss.
Alibi (British Lion) with Margaret Lockwood, Hugh Sinclair, Rodney Ackland, Raymond Lovell; dir: Brian Desmond Hurst.
Secret Mission (Excelsior) with Hugh Williams, Roland Culver, Michael Wilding, Stewart Granger, Herbert Lom; dir: Harold French.
Thunder Rock (MGM) with Michael Redgrave, Lilli Palmer, Finlay Currie, Barry Morse, Miles Malleson; dir: Roy Boulting.

1943   *The Bells Go Down* (Ealing) with Tommy Trinder, Mervyn Johns, Meriel Forbes, Philip Friend, William Hartnell, dir: Basil Dearden.
The Man in Grey (Gainsborough) with Margaret Lockwood, Phyllis Calvert, Stewart Granger, Raymond Lovell; dir: Leslie Arliss.
They Met in the Dark (Excelsior) with Joyce Howard, Tom Walls, Finlay Currie; dir: Karel Lamac.
Candlelight in Algeria (British Lion) with Carla Lehmann, Raymond Lovell, Lea Seidl; dir: George King.

1944   *Fanny By Gaslight* (Gainsborough) with Phyllis Calvert, Stewart Granger, Wilfred Lawson, Jean Kent, Margaretta Scott; dir: Anthony Asquith.

Hotel Reserve (RKO) with Lucie Mannheim, Herbert Lom, Patricia Medina; dir: Victor Hanbury, Lance Comfort and Max Greene.

1945   *A Place of One's Own* (Gainsborough) with Margaret Lockwood, Barbara Mullen, Dennis Price, Dulcie Gray; dir: Bernard Knowles.
They Were Sisters (Gainsborough) with Phyllis Calvert, Hugh Sinclair, Dulcie Gray, Pamela Kellino; dir: Arthur Crabtree.
The Wicked Lady (Gainsborough) with Margaret Lockwood, Patricia Roc, Griffith Jones, Michael Rennie; dir: Leslie Arliss.
The Seventh Veil (Box/GFD) with Ann Todd, Herbert Lom, Hugh McDermott; dir: Compton Bennett.

1947   *Odd Man Out* (Two Cities) with Robert Newton, Robert Beatty, Fay Compton, Kathleen Ryan, Cyril Cusack; dir: Carol Reed.
The Upturned Glass (Box/GFD) with Pamela Kellino, Rosamund John, Maurice Denham; dir: Lawrence Huntington.

1949   *Caught* (MGM) with Barbara Bel Geddes, Robert Ryan, Natalie Schaefer; dir: Max Ophuls.
Madame Bovary (MGM) with Jennifer Jones, Van Heflin, Louis Jourdan, Gladys Cooper; dir: Vincente Minnelli.
The Reckless Moment (Columbia) with Joan Bennett, Geraldine Brooks, Sheppard Strudwick; dir: Max Ophuls.
East Side, West Side (MGM) with Barbara Stanwyck, Ava Gardner, Van Heflin, Cyd Charisse, Nancy Davis; dir: Mervyn LeRoy.

1950   *One Way Street* (Universal) with Marta Toren, Dan Duryea, William Conrad; dir: Hugo Fregonese.

1951   *Pandora and the Flying Dutchman* (MGM) with Ava Gardner, Nigel Patrick, Pamela Kellino, Marius Goring; dir: Albert Lewin.
The Desert Fox (Twentieth Century-Fox) with Cedric Hardwicke, Jessica Tandy, Luther Adler, Richard Boone; dir: Henry Hathaway.

1952   *Five Fingers* (Twentieth Century-Fox) with Dannielle

Darrieux, Michael Rennie, Walter Hampden; dir: Joseph L. Mankiewicz.

The Lady Possessed (Portland) with June Havoc, Pamela Kellino, Fay Compton; dir: Roy Kellino and William Spier.

The Prisoner of Zenda (MGM) with Stewart Granger, Deborah Kerr, Louis Calhern, Robert Douglas, Jane Greer; dir: Richard Thorpe.

Face to Face (RKO) with Michael Pate, Gene Lockhart; dir: John Brahm.

1953   *Charade* (Portland) with Pamela Mason, Scott Forbes, Paul Cavanagh; dir: Roy Kellino.

The Desert Rats (Twentieth Century Fox) with Richard Burton, Robert Newton, Robert Douglas, Torin Thatcher; dir: Robert Wise.

Julius Caesar (MGM) with John Gielgud, Marlon Brando, Greer Garson, Deborah Kerr, Louis Calhern; dir: Joseph L. Mankiewicz.

The Story of Three Loves (MGM) with Moira Shearer, Agnes Moorehead; dir: Gottfried Reinhardt.

Botany Bay (Paramount) with Alan Ladd, Cedric Hardwicke, Patricia Medina; dir: John Farrow.

The Man Between (London Films) with Claire Bloom, Hildegarde Neff, Geoffrey Toone; dir: Carol Reed.

The Tell-Tale Heart (Columbia) dir: Ted Parmelee (animation).

1954   *The Child* (Portland) with Pamela Mason, Portland Mason, Sean McClory; dir: James Mason.

Prince Valiant (Twentieth Century Fox) with Robert Wagner, Janet Leigh, Debra Paget, Sterling Hayden, Brian Aherne; dir: Henry Hathaway.

A Star is Born (Warner) with Judy Garland, Jack Carson, Charles Bickford; dir: George Cukor.

20,000 Leagues Under The Sea (Buena Vista) with Kirk Douglas, Peter Lorre, Paul Lukas; dir: Richard Fleischer.

1956   *Forever Darling* (MGM) with Lucille Ball, Desi Arnaz, Louis Calhern; dir: Alexander Hall.

Bigger Than Life (Twentieth Century Fox) with Barbara Rush, Walter Matthau, Portland Mason; dir: Nicholas Ray.

184

Island in the Sun (Twentieth Century Fox) with Joan Fontaine, Joan Collins, Dorothy Dandridge, Harry Belafonte; dir: Robert Rossen.

1958   *Cry Terror* (MGM) with Rod Steiger, Inger Stevens, Angie Dickinson; dir: Andrew L. Stone.
The Decks Ran Red (MGM) with Dorothy Dandridge, Broderick Crawford, Stuart Whitman; dir: Andrew L. Stone.

1959   *North By Northwest* (MGM) with Cary Grant, Eva Marie Saint, Martin Landau, Jessie Royce Landis; dir: Alfred Hitchcock.
Journey to the Centre of the Earth (Twentieth Century Fox) with Pat Boone, Arlene Dahl, Diane Baker; dir: Henry Levin.
A Touch of Larceny (Paramount) with George Sanders, Vera Miles; dir: Guy Hamilton.

1960   *The Trials of Oscar Wilde* (Warwick) with Peter Finch, Yvonne Mitchell, Nigel Patrick, Lionel Jeffries; dir: Ken Hughes.

1961   *The Marriage-Go-Round* (Twentieth Century Fox) with Susan Hayward, Julie Newmar: dir: Walter Lang.

1962   *Escape From Zahrein* (Paramount) with Yul Brynner, Sal Mineo, Madlyn Rhue; dir: Ronald Neame.
Hero's Island (Portland) with Neville Brand, Rip Torn, Morgan Mason; dir: Leslie Stevens.
Lolita (MGM) with Sue Lyon, Peter Sellers, Shelley Winters; dir: Stanley Kubrick.
Tiara Tahiti (Rank) with John Mills, Claude Dauphin, Herbert Lom; dir: Ted Kotcheff.

1964   *Torpedo Bay* (British Lion) with Lilli Palmer, Alberto Lupo; dir: Bruno Valiati.
The Fall of the Roman Empire (Paramount) with Sophia Loren, Stephen Boyd, Christopher Plummer, Alec Guinness; dir: Anthony Mann.
The Pumpkin Eater (Columbia) with Anne Bancroft, Peter Finch, Cedric Hardwicke, Maggie Smith; dir: Jack Clayton.

1965   *Lord Jim* (Columbia) with Peter O'Toole, Curt Jurgens, Eli Wallach, Jack Hawkins; dir: Richard Brooks.

Genghis Khan (Columbia) with Omar Sharif, Françoise Dorleac, Robert Morley, Telly Savalas; dir: Henry Levin.
Les Pianos Méchaniques (Francos Film) with Hardy Kruger, Melina Mercouri; dir: Juan Antonio Bardem.

1966   *The Blue Max* (Twentieth Century Fox) with George Peppard, Ursula Andress, Jeremy Kemp; dir: John Guillermin.
Georgy Girl (Columbia) with Lynn Redgrave, Alan Bates, Charlotte Rampling; dir: Silvio Narrizzano.
The Deadly Affair (Columbia) with Simone Signoret, Maximilian Schell, Lynn Redgrave, Corin Redgrave, Harry Andrews; dir: Sidney Lumet.

1967   *Stranger in the House* (Rank) with Geraldine Chaplin, Bobby Darin, Ian Ogilvy; dir: Pierre Rouve.
The London Nobody Knows (British Lion) dir: Norman Cohen.

1968   *Duffy* (Columbia) with James Fox, James Coburn, Susannah York; dir: Robert Parrish.
Mayerling (Warner) with Omar Sharif, Catherine Deneuve, Ava Gardner, Genevieve Page; dir: Terence Young.

1969   *Age of Consent* (Columbia) with Helen Mirren, Jack MacGowran, Clarissa Kaye; dir: Michael Powell.
The Sea Gull (Warner) with Vanessa Redgrave, Simone Signoret, David Warner, Harry Andrews, Denholm Elliott; dir: Sidney Lumet.

1970   *Spring and Port Wine* (EMI) with Susan George, Diana Coupland; dir: Peter Hammond.

1971   *Cold Sweat* (EMI) with Charles Bronson, Jill Ireland, Liv Ullmann; dir: Terence Young

1972   *The Yin and Yang of Mr Go* (Ross International) with Burgess Meredith, Jeff Bridges, Broderick Crawford; dir: Burgess Meredith.
Bad Man's River (Scotia International) with Lee Van Cleef, Gina Lollobrigida; dir: Eugenio Martin.
Kill! (Salkind) with Jean Seberg, Stephen Boyd, Curt Jurgens; dir: Romain Gary.

1973   *Child's Play* (Paramount) with Robert Preston, Beau Bridges, Kate Harrington; dir: Sidney Lumet.
The Last of Sheila (Warner) with Richard Benjamin, Dyan Cannon, James Coburn, Joan Hackett, Raquel Welch; dir: Herbert Ross.
The Mackintosh Man (Warner) with Paul Newman, Dominique Sanda, Harry Andrews, Ian Bannen; dir: John Huston.
Frankenstein: The True Story (Universal) with Leonard Whiting, David McCallum, Jane Seymour, Nicola Pagett, Ralph Richardson, John Gielgud; dir: Jack Smight.

1974   *Eleven Harrowhouse* (Twentieth Century Fox) with Candice Bergen, Trevor Howard, John Gielgud, Charles Grodin; dir: Aram Avakian.
The Marseilles Contract (Warner) with Michael Caine, Anthony Quinn; dir: Robert Parrish.
Great Expectations (Transcontinental) with Michael York, Sarah Miles, Margaret Leighton, Robert Morley; dir: Joseph Hardy.

1975   *Inside Out* (Warner) with Telly Savalas, Robert Culp, Aldo Ray; dir: Peter Duffell.
Mandingo (Paramount) with Susan George, Perry King; dir: Richard Fleischer.
Autobiography of a Princess (Merchant/Ivory) with Madhur Jaffrey, Keith Varnier; dir: James Ivory.
La Città Sconvolta (Gastaldi Film) with Valentina Cortese, Mariano Mose; dir: Fernando di Leo.
Gente Di Rispetto (Zampa Film) with Franco Nero, Jennifer O'Neill; dir: Luigi Zampa.
La Mano Sinistra Delle Legge (Rosati Film) with Stephen Boyd, Leonard Mann; dir: Giuseppe Rosati.

1976   *Paura in Città* (Rosati Film) with Cyril Cusack, Raymond Pellegrin; dir: Giuseppe Rosati.
Voyage of the Damned (Avco Embassy) with Faye Dunaway, Max von Sydow, Orson Welles, Oskar Werner, Malcolm McDowell, Ben Gazzarra, Wendy Hiller, Sam Wanamaker, Janet Suzman; dir: Stuart Rosenberg.

1977   *Jesus of Nazareth* (ITC/RAI) with Robert Powell, Anne Bancroft, Ernest Borgnine; dir: Franco Zeffirelli.
Cross of Iron (Avco-Embassy) with James Coburn, Maximilian Schell, David Warner; dir: Sam Peckinpah.
Homage to Chagall (Rasky Film) dir: Harry Rasky.

1978   *Heaven Can Wait* (Paramount) with Warren Beatty, Julie Christie, Dyan Cannon; dir: Warren Beatty and Buck Henry.
The Boys From Brazil (Twentieth Century Fox) with Gregory Peck, Laurence Olivier, Lilli Palmer; dir: Franklin J. Schaffner.
The Water Babies (Ariadne Films) with Billie Whitelaw, David Tomlinson, Joan Greenwood; dir: Lionel Jeffries.
The Passage (Hemdale) with Anthony Quinn, Patricia Neal, Malcolm McDowell; dir: J. Lee Thompson.

1979   *Bloodline* (Paramount) with Audrey Hepburn, Ben Gazzarra, Omar Sharif, Irene Papas; dir: Terence Young.
Murder By Decree (EMI) with Christopher Plummer, David Hemmings, Anthony Quayle, John Gielgud, Frank Finlay; dir: Bob Clark.
Salem's Lot (Warner) with David Soul, Bonnie Bedelia, Lew Ayres, Clarissa Kaye; dir: Tobe Hooper.

1980   *North Sea Hijack* (Universal) with Roger Moore, Anthony Perkins, Faith Brook; dir: Andrew V. McLaglen.

1982   *Ivanhoe* (Columbia) with Anthony Andrews, Sam Neill, Michael Hordern, Olivia Hussey; dir: Douglas Camfield.
Evil Under The Sun (Universal) with Peter Ustinov, Jane Birkin, Colin Blakely; dir: Guy Hamilton.
The Verdict (Twentieth Century Fox) with Paul Newman, Jack Warden, Charlotte Rampling; dir: Sidney Lumet.

1983   *Yellowbeard* (Hemdale) with Marty Feldman, Graham Chapman, Eric Idle, John Cleese; dir: Mel Damski.
Alexandre (Productions Télé-Suisse Romande) with Didier Sauvegrain, Michel Volta; dir: Jean-François Amiguet.
The Assisi Underground (Cannon) with Ben Cross, Irene Papas, Maximilian Schell; dir: Alexander Ramati.

1984   *The Shooting Party* (Edenflow/Reeve) with Edward Fox, John Gielgud, Robert Hardy, Cheryl Campbell, Dorothy Tutin, Gordon Jackson; dir: Alan Bridges.

Radio and Television

James Mason made very few radio appearances except in interviews, though he did play in the occasional BBC radio drama before the war and in 1947 was a regular guest on the Fred Allen comedy shows in New York, where he also hosted and sometimes played in the Lux Radio Theatre. He also read many books for record and tape, and made LP recordings of favourite poems as well as of tales by Edgar Allan Poe.

He made his television debut in 1939 in a series of live BBC dramas from Alexandra Palace, returning to the medium in California in the middle 1950s to host the *Lux Video Theatre* and the *James Mason Show*, both of which were thirty-minute drama series. His other television appearances included regular Bible readings for Yorkshire's *Stars on Sunday* series in the 1970s, while he also narrated the Thames Television documentary series *Hollywood* and the BBC's *Search for the Nile*. His other television appearances as an actor in Britain and America included:

1957   *Marooned*; *The Questioning Note*; *The Thundering Wave*; *Not the Glory*.

1959   *The Second Man*; *A Sword for Marius*; *The Hiding Place*; *Once Upon a Knight*.

1960   *John Brown's Body*.

1962   *Tonight in Samarkand*; *Rebecca*; *Captive Audience*.

1965   *Doctor Kildare* (four episodes).

1966   *Dare I Weep, Dare I Mourn*.

1968   *The Legend of Silent Night*.

1969   *The Tormentors*; *A Tall Stalwart Lancer*.

1983   *Anno Domini*, *George Washington*.

1984   *Dr Fischer of Geneva*.

Index

191

194

Mason, Colin (brother), 8, 9

Mason, James: birth and family background, 7–8; at prep and public school, 8–11; and exclusion from family business, 9; at university, 12–16; and student theatre, 13–15; first-class degree in architecture, 14, 15, 16; decision to become actor, 16, 17; professional début in touring productions, 18, 19–21, 22–3; in repertory, 23–4; London début, 24; Old Vic season, 24, 25–7, 29, 34, 38; brief West End season, 27–8; sacking from Korda film, 28, 32, 33; returns to theatre, 29–31, 36, 37, 38, 39, 41–2, 46, 48, 51; unemployment, 31–2, 46; screen début, 32, 33; in quota quickies, 32, 34, 35, 36; first meeting with Pamela, 35, 37; joins Kellino household, 35, 38–9, 45, 47, 49, 51, 59; dissatisfaction with career, 38–9, 40–41, 43, 48, 114, 119, 120; criticism of British film policy, 40; private movie-making, 44–6; turns to television, 49; pacifism and decision to become conscientious objector, 49–50, 51, 64, 83, 115, 121; rift with family, 49, 77; as poultry farmer, 52; marriage, 53; last West End stage appearance, 53; first notable movie, 53–4; intense screen activity, 54–8; in costume melodramas, 56–8, 60, 61–2, 70; as international film star 57, 61; 'man you love to hate' label, 57, 60; contempt for British films, 57–8, 62–3, 64–5, 69, 70, 73, 74, 77, 154; 'difficult' reputation, 58, 68, 69, 78, 82–3; controversial articles, 62–3, 64–5, 68, 70; successes, 67–8, 69, 70–72, 103; emigration to America, 74–6, 77; breach-of-contract suit, 76, 77–8, 79, 81, 82, 87; damaging reconstruction of career, 75–6, 77–8, 88; failure of Broadway début, 78–9; journalism and radio shows, 79–81; move to Hollywood, 82; loathing for Los Angeles, 83; as a loner, 83, 85, 90, 150; failure of freelance art films, 83–4, 85, 88–9; unconventional living arrangements, 84–5, 87, 93, 94, 116; criticism of US studios and British colony, 85, 89, 98–9; further lawsuits, 87, 115, 121; decision to seek American citizenship, 89, 90, 103; filming in Britain, 89–90, 103, 124, 126, 127; unpopularity, 90; joint projects with Pamela, 92–3, 96, 115; first Hollywood success and golden period, 92, 93, 95, 96, 99–100; move to Keaton home, 94; television projects, 96, 97–8, 115; doldrums, 102, 103, 120; reconciliation with family, 103, 124; triumph in *A Star is Born*, 105–6, 108; Oscar nominations, 106, 142, 154, 171, 172; return to classical theatre, 109–12, 113, 169–70; farewell to hope of becoming classical actor, 112, 114, 133, 151, 157; realization of errors in career, 114, 119, 120, 132, 134, 136, 138, 144, 153–4; as producer, 116, 118; disintegrating marriage, 119, 122, 123, 127, 128, 133, 134; summer-stock seasons, 120; in supporting character roles, 121–2, 123–4, 130, 131–2, 139, 141, 142, 143, 161, 162; woman friends, 122, 125, 127–8, 136–7, 143, 146, 174; as light comedian, 124–5, 126, 127; desire to return to Europe, 126, 127, 128, 134, 135; singing and dancing lessons, 131; return to critical acclaim, 132, 135, 160, 169–70, 171–3, 175; divorce, 134, 136, 138–9; financial burden, 135, 138–9, 153; pot-boiling films, 137–8, 139–40; move to Switzerland, 139; increasingly important roles, 141–3; as jobbing actor, 143, 144, 147, 152–3; at film festivals, 144; as co-producer, 147–8; friendship with Clarissa, 147–9, 150, 153–4; attempt at autobiography, 149–50; refusal of National Theatre offer, 151; multinational films, 152, 153, 155, 159–62, 163; marriage, 155; as television Bible reader, 156; settled life with Clarissa, 159, 162, 166, 170–1, 174; return to Hollywood, 163–5; last assault on Broadway, 166–8; ill-health, 172–3, 175; final triumph in *Shooting Party*, 175; death, 176

Mason, John (father), 7, 9, 12, 14, 128

O'Dea, Dennis, 72
O'Herlihy, Dan, 71
O'Neill, Eugene, 26
O'Toole, Peter, 139, 157
Oberon Merle, 41
Observer, 61, 72, 88, 91, 118
Odd Man Out, 44, 71–2, 73, 74, 78, 103, 131
Odets, Clifford, 116
Oedipus Rex (Sophocles), 109, 110, 111, 133
Ogilvy, Ian, 144
Old Heidelberg (Mayer-Foster), 21
Old Vic, 24, 25–7, 29, 34
Olivier, Laurence, 27, 31, 39, 61, 114, 158, 164; offers Mason role in National Theatre film, 151
On the Waterfront, 106
One Way Street, 88, 89
Ophuls, Max, 83, 88
Osborn, Andrew, 50, 51
Oscar, Henry, 41
Othello (Shakespeare), 30

Pandora and the Flying Dutchman, 89, 90, 91–2
Papas, Irene, 164
Paramount, 75
Parker, Al, 32, 34, 35, 43, 47, 48, 56
Parker, Cecil, 41
Parker, Maggie (Margaret Johnston), 32, 48, 132
Parnell (Schauffler), 36
Parsons, Louella, 78
Partridge in a Pear Tree (Stevens), 168
Pascal, Gabriel, 50, 51
Passage, The, 162
Pathé, 52
Patrick, Nigel, 91
Paura in Città, 161
Peck, Gregory, 164
People, 90
Peppard, George, 141
Perkins, Anthony, 158, 159, 169
Pianos Mécaniques, Les, 140
Pinter, Harold, 138
Place of One's Own, A, 60
Plummer, Christopher, 137, 164, 165
Poe, Edgar Allan, 102
Portland Productions, 92, 130
Portman, Eric, 56, 61

Powell, Dilys, 54, 138
Powell, Michael, 66, 147, 148, 149, 157
Pressburger, Emeric, 66
Preston, Robert, 97
Previn, André, 157
Price, Vincent, 31
Pride and Prejudice (Longford), 39
Prince Valiant, 103
Prison Breaker, 35
Prisoner of Zenda, The (Rose), 23
Prisoner of Zenda, The, 96–7, 102
Provok'd Wife, The (Vanbrugh), 30
Pumpkin Eater, The, 128, 129
Purcell, Henry, 15
Purdom, Edmund, 113

Quartermaine, Leon, 25
Quayle, Anthony, 137, 158
Queen of Scots, (Daviot), 27–8, 29, 31
Quinn, Anthony, 161
Quintero, Jose, 167

Radio City, 172
Radio City Rockettes, 171
Raimu, 144
Rainer, Luise, 40
Rains, Claude, 83, 163
Rank, J. Arthur, 74, 76, 77, 88
Rank Organization, 46, 60; five-picture contract with, 55–8; Mason's contempt for, 57–8, 65, 70; Mason's attacks on, 62, 74, 77; severed connections with, 80
Rascal, The (Kevnov), 18
Rave magazine, 115
Ray, Nicholas, 116
Reagan, Nancy, 88, 117, 170
Reagan, Ronald, 88, 117, 170
Reckless Moment, The, 88, 90
Red Badge of Courage, The, 87
Redgrave, Lynn, 141, 142
Redgrave, Michael, 14, 54–5, 65
Redgrave, Vanessa, 151
Reed, Carol, 71, 72, 103
Reed, Rex, 159
Reinhardt, Wolfgang, 83
Rembrandt, 27
Rendel, Robert, 34
Rennie, Michael, 121
Return of Don Juan, The, 27, 28, 32
Return of the Scarlet Pimpernel, The, 41